**LOUIS B. WRIGHT**, General Editor. Director of the Folger Shakespeare Library from 1948 until his retirement in 1968, Dr. Wright has devoted over forty years to the study of the Shakespearean period. In 1926 he completed his doctoral thesis on "Vaudeville Elements in Elizabethan Drama" and subsequently published many articles on the stagecraft and theatre of Shakespeare's day. He is the author of *Middle-Class Culture in Elizabethan England* (1935), *Religion and Empire* (1942), *The Elizabethans' America* (1965), and many other books and essays on the history and literature of the Tudor and Stuart periods, including *Shakespeare for Everyman* (1964). Dr. Wright has taught at the universities of North Carolina, California at Los Angeles, Michigan, Minnesota, and other American institutions. From 1932 to 1948 he was instrumental in developing the research program of the Henry E. Huntington Library and Art Gallery. During his tenure as Director, the Folger Shakespeare Library became one of the leading research institutions of the world for the study of the backgrounds of Anglo-American civilization.

**VIRGINIA A. LaMAR**, Assistant Editor. A member of the staff of the Folger Shakespeare Library from 1946 until her death in 1968, Miss LaMar served as research assistant to the Director and as Executive Secretary. Prior to 1946 Miss LaMar had been a secretary in the British Admiralty Delegation in Washington, D.C., receiving the King's Medal in 1945 for her services. She was coeditor of the *Historie of Travell into Virginia Britania* by William Strachey, published by The Hakluyt Society in 1953, and author of *English Dress in the Age of Shakespeare* and *Travel and Roads in England* in the "Folger Booklets on Tudor and Stuart Civilization" series.

## The Folger Shakespeare Library

*The Folger Library General Reader's Shakespeare*

THE TRAGEDY OF

# HAMLET,

PRINCE OF DENMARK

By

# WILLIAM
# SHAKESPEARE

**WASHINGTON SQUARE PRESS**
POCKET BOOKS • NEW YORK

# THE TRAGEDY OF HAMLET,
## PRINCE OF DENMARK

WASHINGTON SQUARE PRESS edition published February, 1958

37th printing.....................August, 1976

A new edition of a distinguished
literary work now made available in
an inexpensive, well-designed format

Published by
POCKET BOOKS, a division of Simon & Schuster, Inc.,
A GULF+WESTERN COMPANY
630 Fifth Avenue, New York, N.Y. 10020.

WASHINGTON SQUARE PRESS editions are distrib-
uted in the U.S. by Simon & Schuster, Inc., 630 Fifth
Avenue, New York, N.Y. 10020, and in Canada by Simon
& Schuster of Canada, Ltd., Markham, Ontario, Canada.

## Preface

This edition of *Hamlet* is designed to make available a readable text of one of Shakespeare's greatest plays. In the centuries since Shakespeare many changes have occurred in the meanings of words, and some clarification of Shakespeare's vocabulary may be helpful. To provide the reader with necessary notes in the most accessible format, we have placed them on the pages facing the text that they explain. We have tried to make these notes as brief and simple as possible. Preliminary to the text we have also included a brief statement of essential information about Shakespeare and his stage. Readers desiring more detailed information should refer to the books suggested in the references, and if still further information is needed, the bibliographies in those books will provide the necessary clues to the literature of the subject.

L. B. W.
V. A. L.

*August 15, 1957*

## THE POPULARITY OF

# *Hamlet*

Of all the plays written by Shakespeare, *Hamlet* has enjoyed the greatest popularity. It was a success when it was first performed, probably about 1600, and it has had constant revivals through the centuries. The title role is one that most actors aspire to play and they regard success in that part as the ultimate achievement of a career. This play has been translated into many languages and it is familiar to theatregoers throughout the world. Almost any literate schoolboy in Europe, Africa, Asia, or the Americas will be able to recognize the source of the soliloquy beginning "To be, or not to be," and numerous quotations from the play have become clichés of everyday speech. No college yearbook can go to press without printing under some of the photographs a descriptive line from *Hamlet* such as "The glass of fashion and the mould of form."

Literary critics and academic commentators have found in *Hamlet* themes for endless disquisitions. More has been written about *Hamlet* than about any other single drama. It has inspired profound and philosophic reasoning, and it has also set off an explosion of nonsense that has made almost impenetrable the dusty smog of Shakespearean criticism. A bibliography of books, essays, articles, and notes on *Hamlet* would fill a volume. After reading *Hamlet*, apparently only the most determined souls can resist seizing a pen or racing for their typewriters to set down their explanations of the character of the Prince of Denmark, which to some writers is a mystery past unraveling, but not a mystery that leaves them silent. To one learned German critic the explanation of Hamlet's vacillation was easy. According to his theory, the chief protagonist was not really a prince but a woman who could not make up her mind. Everybody can find in this play something to stimulate his speculative nature and stir his imagination. For nearly two centuries scholars and critics have been arguing over every aspect of the play, ranging from textual problems to the philosophic meaning that Shakespeare meant to convey. Needless to say, they have not reached agreement, but they have enjoyed the controversies.

Some tons of white paper and much printer's ink might have been saved if commentators had studied with greater care theatrical conditions, conventions of the drama, public taste, and social attitudes in Shakespeare's England. For, as Shakespeare portrays him, Hamlet is an Elizabethan, adapted to the requirements of dramatic fashion, and not a medieval Dane, as literal historians would make him out. And he is distinctly not a Victorian gentleman created in the image of Albert, the Prince Consort, as Edward Dowden and even later critics would represent him. No amount of moralizing about how a Victorian Englishman or a twentieth-century American would react to the circumstances in which Hamlet found himself will explain what Shakespeare intended his character to represent. Nevertheless, such is Shakespeare's genius in the portrayal of character that every generation can see in Hamlet and in the other major figures in the play universal qualities

that persist from age to age. The timeless humanity of
the play is the quality that has given it enduring popularity on the stage and in the library.

## THE HAMLET "PROBLEM"

Much of the vast literature on this play has concentrated on the interpretation of Hamlet's character, particularly in attempting to explain his inability to take
decisive action, his treatment of Ophelia, his madness,
real or feigned, and a host of other questions called up
by his actions. These constitute the "Hamlet problem."
The answer is to be found in the study of Shakespeare's
play as a piece for the public stage at the end of the
sixteenth century rather than in subjecting Hamlet himself to psychoanalysis. Actually, Shakespeare's audience
was not aware of a "Hamlet problem," and nobody for
more than a century and a half worried about possible
faults in Hamlet's character that made him put off killing Claudius. When someone finally raised the question
of Hamlet's delay, an eighteenth-century critic, Thomas
Hanmer, remarked that if the Prince had gone "naturally to work" in the first act, the play would have ended
right there. When Shakespeare's audience went to the
Globe in 1600, they expected to see a rousing melo-
drama in the popular genre of the revenge tragedy, and
that is precisely what Shakespeare set out to give them,
a play full of all the conventional trappings that audiences had learned to expect, including a great deal of
suspense until the violent denouement of the last act.
If *Hamlet* transcends the run-of-the-mill revenge play,
that again is further proof of its author's genius; but
one should always remember that Shakespeare was a

practical man with an extraordinary sense of what is "good theatre" and that he always wrote with both eyes on the box office and never a glance toward posterity in Academia, a destiny that would have appalled him.

Because *Hamlet* is a well-made revenge play designed to appeal to the taste of an Elizabethan audience that had whetted its appetite on the sensations served up in Thomas Kyd's *Spanish Tragedy*, Shakespeare's own *Titus Andronicus*, and an earlier but now lost *Tragedy of Hamlet*, it does not follow that it lacked the qualities of greatness. The most enduring plays have always been those that made a popular appeal in the theatre. "Intellectual" closet dramas have remained just there—in the closet. Shakespeare in *Hamlet* shows an understanding of human life and character that had deepened with his own maturity, and he expressed that knowledge in poetry that has become a part of the world's heritage of great literature. Proof of the permanent literary value of the play lies in its popularity as a work to be read. Thousands of persons who have never had an opportunity to see it on the stage have read it with pleasure and profit.

Much of the delight of modern readers, of course, comes from the study of the characters of the principal figures in the play, for Shakespeare has presented them in three-dimensional vividness. We feel that they are living beings with problems that are perennially human. If a modern man is not called upon, as Hamlet was, to avenge a murdered father, he nevertheless must face crises in his own life that remind him of Hamlet's dilemma, and he recognizes in the mental attitudes of the various persons of the play attitudes that are familiar in everyday life. Everybody has encountered an Ophelia, a sweet but uninspiring girl dominated by her father and brother. And everybody has had to put up with a Polonius, full of conceit over his worldly wisdom and ever ready to advise us with an unctuous cliché.

Inevitably, the modern reader's interest concentrates on the character of Hamlet himself. The play, after all, is about his problems, and the unusual care that Shakespeare took in writing his lines shows his own concern with the interpretation of that part. We may be sure, however, that Shakespeare never intended to present Hamlet as a delicate flower, too intellectual and sensitive to cope with the rude milieu of the Danish court—an interpretation that Romantic critics of the nineteenth century sometimes favored. Hamlet was no Bunthorne and would not have "walked down Piccadilly with a lily in his hand." On the contrary, Hamlet reflected in his character qualities that an Englishman in 1600 would have understood as those to be expected in a prince who had been educated to rule his country. From what others say of him in the course of the action, we know that Hamlet's melancholic attitude when the play opens is not normal for him and that he was not characteristically ineffectual in action. At his best, he possessed qualities and abilities typical of the Renaissance ideal of the gentleman: courage, generosity, learning, wit, courtly bearing, skill with the sword, and a taste for music and drama. Only since his father's death has he succumbed to melancholy which has temporarily made him apathetic and slow to act.

In discussing the meaning of *Hamlet* in Elizabethan terms, Miss Lily Bess Campbell in *Shakespeare's Tragic Heroes* shows with much plausibility that Shakespeare is intent upon studying the effects of grief, not only upon Hamlet but, with contrasting effect, upon Laertes and Fortinbras, who suffer analogous losses. She demonstrates from contemporary evidence the notion that inconsolable grief such as Hamlet experienced after the shock of his father's death left the victim lethargic and inactive. But there is more to Shakespeare's treatment than this. The play and the characterizations are both complex, and the very complexity has proved one of its fascinations for readers who like to dissect the personalities of the characters involved.

Hamlet, possessed of a finely trained intellect, is a man with a philosophic approach to life. He has been at the University of Wittenberg, where he has engaged in the subtleties of intellectual speculation. By training, such a man learns to analyze problems, and his responses are never automatic because his decisions come after contemplation rather than from impulse. Though he may be slow to make a decision, that decision will be based on reason.

Shakespeare's age was fond of debating the relative merits of the contemplative versus the active life. The ideal of education was a proper balance between the two, and the ideal courtier, exemplified in a person like Sir Philip Sidney, demonstrated both aspects. By implication, and by the words of other characters, Shakespeare gives Hamlet qualities familiar in the best of the Renaissance Englishmen. Though he did not neglect the active life, he found his greatest pleasure in the cultivation of his mind. Such a man, brought back to the sordid realities of the Danish court, might well complain against the cursed spite of fate that forced him to set right the evils around him. Complain though he might, he would not neglect his duty. Instead, he would study the problems before him and attempt their solution when he had satisfied his reason. If Hamlet's methods of working out his problems are indirect and time-consuming, he is merely following the pattern of behavior of the thoughtful and speculative type of thinker.

A part of Hamlet's agony results from the very fact that he has a keen and alert mind that sees the implication of any potential action. When he finds Claudius at his prayers, he does not take his revenge by stabbing him but delays for a more fitting time. Had he reacted automatically, as the choleric Laertes would have done, he would have killed Claudius and realized too late that he had slain him in a moment of repentance and given him the rewards of heaven. The killing of Claudius would be an act of finality, but Hamlet, with his idealism so wounded by his knowledge of the evil surrounding him, was inhibited by his awareness that Claudius' death would not restore his own faith in the innate goodness of human life.

Hamlet's qualities may be seen in many intellectual figures who enter public life and are brought face to face with the realities of practical politics. The happy politician is one who, unhampered by a philosophic mind, can respond automatically in accordance with the required conventions of behavior. The speculative thinker finds it difficult to react instantly and decisively in political crises. Perhaps one reason for the popularity of Hamlet is the sympathy which all thoughtful and studious persons must feel for the Prince, and their self-identification with his type.

## SOURCE AND TEXT OF THE PLAY

The plot of *Hamlet* comes ultimately from Saxo Grammaticus' *Historia Danica*, a twelfth-century chronicle first printed in Paris in 1514, but Shakespeare did not take his plot directly from this source. The tale was included in the 1570's in François de Belleforest's *Histoires Tragiques*, a French collection of short stories, and it was the subject of a play acted in London as early as 1587–1589. Thomas Lodge in 1596 alludes to "the ghost which cried so miserably at the Theatre, like an oyster wife, 'Hamlet, revenge!'" Shakespeare apparently based his play, first acted about 1600, upon the older play, which evidently was never printed.

A play called "the Revenge of Hamlet, Prince of Denmark, as it was lately acted by the Lord Chamberlain his servants" was registered for printing with the Stationers' Company on July 26, 1602. Shakespeare's company at this time was known as the Lord Chamberlain's Men. The next year, 1603, there appeared in print *The Tragical History of Hamlet, Prince of Denmark. By William Shakespeare* and the title added, "As it hath been divers times acted by His Highness' servants in the city of London, as also in the two universities of Cambridge and Oxford and elsewhere." King James I had in the meantime succeeded to the throne, and Shakespeare's company had acquired a royal patron; hence the change to "His Highness' servants." This is the version known as the First Quarto. It is a short and corrupt text. Some changes make it quite different from the accepted text. For example, Polonius and his servant, Reynaldo, are called in Quarto I Corambis and

Montano, many of the speeches are much abbreviated, and the order of scenes varies to some extent.

The next printed version appeared in 1604 and added after the name of the author: "Newly imprinted and enlarged to almost as much again as it was, according to the true and perfect copy." This is the Second Quarto. A Third Quarto appeared in 1611, but this is merely a reprint of Quarto II. The next version of the play was the text published in the First Folio of 1623.

Quarto II provides the fullest version, having more than two hundred lines omitted in the First Folio, but it leaves out about eighty-five lines found in the Folio. Sir Edmund Chambers observes that Quarto II is "a fair text, with little mislineation, light punctuation, and a good many abnormal spellings, and may very possibly be from the author's manuscript, but if so, numerous misprints suggest that this was not very legible. There is no evidence that it had been used as prompt-copy."

Quarto II and the First Folio text, in Chambers' opinion, "show a common origin," but he thinks the copy from which the printers set the First Folio text had been altered for use as a promptbook.

Quarto I, though printed first, has little textual authority and seems to have been put together by some actor from memory; Chambers suggests that "the text of the performances reported in Quarto I derived from the same transcript which underlies [the] F[olio]."

The present editors have followed the usual practice of collating Quarto II and the First Folio to establish their text. In dealing with a Shakespearean text, one should always remember that not even Shakespeare's copy was regarded as Holy Writ, and that it has been the immemorial practice in the theatre for authors,

Queen Elizabeth.
From the Trevelyon MS. (c. 1608).

**King James I.**
From the Trevelyon MS. (c. 1608).

producers, and actors to tinker with the copy, to "edit" the play to suit the circumstances or their whim at the moment. No amount of bibliographical detective work, brilliant as some of it is, can ever determine with finality whether every word is precisely the one that Shakespeare wrote, for we can never know who may have altered a word or a line here and there in the long progress through the playhouse and through the printing press.

## STAGE HISTORY

The first actor to play Hamlet was Shakespeare's friend and colleague Richard Burbage, and since that time nearly every tragedian, including some women and children, have attempted the role with varying degrees of success and popularity. Thomas Betterton, one of the best actors of the Restoration period, received from Sir William Davenant, who revived the play in 1661, an account of the way the part was played by his predecessors; thus he served as a connecting link between the tradition of Shakespeare's stage and later stage practices. Betterton was one of the great Hamlets and continued to play the part effectively until he was seventy. A portrait of Betterton, still hanging in the Garrick Club in London, shows him dressed for his part wearing a dark and somber dress that many later Hamlets regarded as essential to the role. But Betterton also wore a full-bottomed wig and other elements of dress characteristic of the age of Charles II. Neither the actors in Shakespeare's day nor any others until the Romantic period thought of costuming the play to make the characters look like medieval Danes.

David Garrick, the famous actor-manager of the eighteenth century, was noted for his acting of Hamlet, whom he first impersonated in 1742. Some of the stage business that he invented persisted for generations. He began playing the part costumed to look like a prince in the court of his sovereign, George II, and presumably kept up with changing court styles as the years passed. Staging *Hamlet* in modern dress is no innovation of our time.

John Philip Kemble, who began playing Hamlet in 1783, was one of the first to interpret the role romantically and to invest the part with trappings of costume and stage business to emphasize the excessive melancholy of the "gloomy Dane." A portrait painted by Sir Thomas Lawrence shows him standing in a graveyard, dressed in a long black robe and holding poor Yorick's skull. In the background are the battlements of Elsinore. From Kemble's time onward, the gloominess and sometimes the madness of Hamlet received emphasis.

*Hamlet* was popular from an early time in America. In 1759, Lewis Hallam brought a company to Philadelphia with *Hamlet* in their repertoire, and they presented the play elsewhere in the Colonies. From this time onward, *Hamlet*, along with other Shakespearean plays, became a part of the standard dramatic fare that Americans approved. On the American frontier, Shakespeare was always popular and *Hamlet* was one of the favorite plays. Among the American actors of the nineteenth century, the two best-known Hamlets were probably Edwin Forrest and Edwin Booth. English companies of actors constantly toured America and most of the famous English Hamlets were well known on this continent.

Costume of an English gentleman.
From the Trevelyon MS. (c. 1608).

Costume of an English lady.
From the Trevelyon MS. (c. 1608).

Early in the nineteenth century, the English stage was afflicted with a plague of juvenile actors, some of whom were so ill-advised as to attempt Hamlet. Perhaps the most famous of these was Master William Henry West Betty, who, in 1803, at the age of twelve, edified English audiences with his interpretation of the Prince of Denmark. Almost as bad, and in some respects worse, was the interpretation by women actors who usually saw in Hamlet a poor frustrated feminine soul. The most noted female Hamlet was Sarah Bernhardt, who played the part in Paris in 1899 and the next year in New York. Of her performance, William Winter commented that "Hamlet has been roughly handled on the stage, but a long remembrance of his sufferings does not recall a time when he was more effectively crucified than he is in the French play by the French actress."

Among the best-known Hamlets of the later nineteenth century were Sir Henry Irving, Herbert Beerbohm Tree, Sir Johnston Forbes-Robertson, and E. H. Sothern. In more recent years, Maurice Evans, Sir John Gielgud, and Sir Laurence Olivier have achieved distinction in the role. Olivier's screen version, filled with symbolic fog and winding stairs in his shots of Elsinore Castle, attracted considerable attention. The performance of an uncut version of *Hamlet*, directed by Margaret Webster in 1938 for Maurice Evans, proved a surprising success despite its great length, which required an intermission for dinner. Miss Webster's delightful *Shakespeare Without Tears* describes the enduring popularity of *Hamlet* on the stage and emphasizes the continuing vitality of Shakespeare.

Within ten years of Shakespeare's death, an English acting company led by John Green was performing a version of the *Hamlet* play at Dresden, and from that day to this, *Hamlet* has been a favorite with German audiences. Germans have been heard to contend that the Schlegel-Tieck translation of *Hamlet* into German is better than the original. The earliest version of *Hamlet* in German, *Der Bestrafte Brudermord* ("Fratricide Punished"), a corrupt text probably deriving from Quarto II, is dated 1710.

On the stage and in the library, in English-speaking countries and elsewhere, *Hamlet* has attracted enduring interest. A knowledge of this play is essential to every person who makes any pretension to literary cultivation.

## THE AUTHOR

Even before *Hamlet* first appeared in print, Shakespeare was so well known as a literary and dramatic craftsman that Francis Meres, a young preacher, in a volume called *Palladis Tamia: Wits Treasury* (1598), referred in flattering terms to him as "mellifluous and honey-tongued Shakespeare," famous for his *Venus and Adonis*, his *Lucrece*, and "his sugared sonnets," which were circulating "among his private friends." Meres observes further that "as Plautus and Seneca are accounted the best for comedy and tragedy among the Latins, so Shakespeare among the English is the most excellent in both kinds for the stage," and he mentions a dozen plays that had made a name for Shakespeare. He concludes with the remark "that the Muses would speak with Shakespeare's fine filed phrase if they would speak English."

To those acquainted with the history of the Elizabethan and Jacobean periods, it is incredible that any-

one should be so naïve or ignorant as to doubt the
reality of Shakespeare as the author of the plays that
bear his name. Yet so much nonsense has been written
about other "candidates" for the plays that it is well to
remind readers that no credible evidence that would
stand up in a court of law has ever been adduced to
prove either that Shakespeare did not write his plays
or that anyone else wrote them. All the theories offered
for the authorship of Francis Bacon, the Earl of Derby,
the Earl of Oxford, the Earl of Hertford, Christopher
Marlowe, and a score of other candidates are mere conjectures spun from the active imaginations of persons
who confuse hypothesis and conjecture with evidence.

As Meres' statement of 1598 indicates, Shakespeare
was already a popular playwright whose name carried
weight at the box office. The obvious reputation of
Shakespeare as early as 1598 makes the effort to prove
him a myth one of the most absurd in the history of
human perversity.

The anti-Shakespeareans talk darkly about a plot of
vested interests to maintain the authorship of Shakespeare. Nobody has any vested interest in Shakespeare,
but every scholar is interested in the truth and in the
quality of evidence advanced by special pleaders who
set forth hypotheses in place of facts.

The anti-Shakespeareans base their arguments upon
a few simple premises, all of them false. These false
premises are that Shakespeare was an unlettered yokel
without any schooling, that nothing is known about
Shakespeare, and that only a noble lord or the equivalent in background could have written the plays. The
facts are that more is known about Shakespeare than
about most dramatists of his day, that he had a very

good education, acquired in the Stratford Grammar
School, that the plays show no evidence of profound
book learning, and that the knowledge of kings and
courts evident in the plays is no greater than any in-
telligent young man could have picked up at second
hand. Most anti-Shakespeareans are naïve and betray
an obvious snobbery. The author of their favorite plays,
they imply, must have had a college diploma framed
and hung on his study wall, like the one in their den-
tist's office, and obviously so great a writer must have
had a title or some equally significant evidence of ex-
alted social background. They forget that genius has a
way of cropping up in unexpected places and that none
of the great creative writers of the world got his in-
spiration in a college or university course.

William Shakespeare was the son of John Shakespeare
of Stratford-upon-Avon, a substantial citizen of that
small but busy market town in the center of the rich
agricultural county of Warwick. John Shakespeare kept
a shop, what we would call a general store; he dealt
in wool and other produce and gradually acquired property. As a youth, John Shakespeare had learned the
trade of glover and leather worker. There is no contemporary evidence that the elder Shakespeare was a
butcher, though the anti-Shakespeareans like to talk
about the ignorant "butcher's boy of Stratford." Their
only evidence is a statement by gossipy John Aubrey,
more than a century after William Shakespeare's birth,
that young William followed his father's trade, and
when he killed a calf, "he would do it in a high style and
make a speech." We would like to believe the story
true, but Aubrey is not a very credible witness.

John Shakespeare probably continued to operate a

farm at Snitterfield that his father had leased. He married Mary Arden, daughter of his father's landlord, a man of some property. The third of their eight children was William, baptized on April 26, 1564, and probably born three days before. At least, it is conventional to celebrate April 23 as his birthday.

The Stratford records give considerable information about John Shakespeare. We know that he held several municipal offices, including those of alderman and mayor. In 1580 he was in some sort of legal difficulty and was fined for neglecting a summons of the Court of Queen's Bench requiring him to appear at Westminster and be bound over to keep the peace.

As a citizen and alderman of Stratford, John Shakespeare was entitled to send his son to the grammar school free. Though the records are lost, there can be no reason to doubt that this is where young William received his education. As any student of the period knows, the grammar schools provided the basic education in Latin learning and literature. The Elizabethan grammar school is not to be confused with modern grammar schools. Many cultivated men of the day received all their formal education in the grammar schools. At the universities in this period a student would have received little training that would have inspired him to be a creative writer. At Stratford young Shakespeare would have acquired a familiarity with Latin and some little knowledge of Greek. He would have read Latin authors and become acquainted with the plays of Plautus and Terence. Undoubtedly, in this period of his life he received that stimulation to read and explore for himself the world of ancient and modern history that he later utilized in his plays. The youngster who does not acquire this type of intellectual curiosity *before* college days rarely develops as a result of a college course the kind of mind Shakespeare demonstrated. His learning in books was anything but profound, but he clearly had the probing curiosity that sent him in search of information, and he had a keenness in the observation of nature and of humankind that finds reflection in his poetry.

There is little documentation for Shakespeare's boyhood. There is little reason why there should be. Nobody knew that he was going to be a dramatist about whom any scrap of information would be prized in the centuries to come. He was merely an active and vigorous youth of Stratford, perhaps assisting his father in his business, and no Boswell bothered to write down facts about him. The most important record that we have is a marriage license issued by the Bishop of Worcester on November 28, 1582, to permit William Shakespeare to marry Anne Hathaway, seven or eight years his senior; furthermore, the Bishop permitted the marriage after reading the banns only once instead of three times, evidence of the desire for haste. The need was explained on May 26, 1583, when the christening of Susanna, daughter of William and Anne Shakespeare, was recorded at Stratford. Two years later, on February 2, 1585, the records show the birth of twins to the Shakespeares, a boy and a girl who were christened Hamnet and Judith.

What William Shakespeare was doing in Stratford during the early years of his married life, or when he went to London, we do not know. It has been conjectured that he tried his hand at schoolteaching, but that is a mere guess. There is a legend that he left

Stratford to escape a charge of poaching in the park
of Sir Thomas Lucy of Charlecote, but there is no proof
of this. There is also a legend that when first he came
to London, he earned his living by holding horses outside a playhouse and presently was given employment
inside, but there is nothing better than eighteenth-century hearsay for this. How Shakespeare broke into the
London theatres as a dramatist and actor we do not
know. But lack of information is not surprising, for
Elizabethans did not write their autobiographies, and
we know even less about the lives of many writers and
some men of affairs than we know about Shakespeare.
By 1592 he was so well established and popular that
he incurred the envy of the dramatist and pamphleteer
Robert Greene, who referred to him as an "upstart
crow . . . in his own conceit the only Shake-scene in a
country." From this time onward, contemporary allu-
sions and references in legal documents enable the
scholar to chart Shakespeare's career with greater accuracy than is possible with most other Elizabethan
dramatists.

By 1594 Shakespeare was a member of the company
of actors known as the Lord Chamberlain's Men. After
the accession of James I, in 1603, the company would
have the sovereign for their patron and would be known
as the King's Men. During the period of its greatest
prosperity, this company would have as its principal
theatres the Globe and the Blackfriars. Shakespeare was
both an actor and a shareholder in the company. He
thus had three sources of income: from the sale of his
plays to the company, from his wages as an actor, and
from his share of the profits of the theatrical company.
Tradition has assigned him such acting roles as Adam

in *As You Like It* and the Ghost in *Hamlet*, a modest place on the stage that suggests that he may have had other duties in the management of the company. Such conclusions, however, are based on surmise.

What we do know is that his plays were popular and that he was highly successful in his triple vocation. His first play may have been *The Comedy of Errors*, acted perhaps in 1591. Certainly this was one of his earliest plays. The three parts of *Henry VI* were acted sometime between 1590 and 1592. Critics are not in agreement about precisely how much Shakespeare wrote of these three plays. *Richard III* probably dates from 1593. With this play Shakespeare captured the imagination of Elizabethan audiences, then enormously interested in historical plays. With *Richard III*, Shakespeare also gave an interpretation pleasing to the Tudors of the rise to power of the grandfather of Queen Elizabeth. From this time onward, Shakespeare's plays followed on the stage in rapid succession: *Titus Andronicus, The Taming of the Shrew, The Two Gentlemen of Verona, Love's Labour's Lost, Romeo and Juliet, Richard II, A Midsummer Night's Dream, King John, The Merchant of Venice, Henry IV*, Pts. I and II, *Much Ado About Nothing, Henry V, Julius Cæsar, As You Like It, Twelfth Night, Hamlet, The Merry Wives of Windsor, All's Well That Ends Well, Measure for Measure, Othello, King Lear*, and nine others that followed before Shakespeare retired completely, about 1613.

In the course of his career in London, he made enough money to enable him to return to Stratford with a competence. His purchase on May 4, 1597, of New Place, then the second-largest dwelling in Stratford, a "pretty house of brick and timber," with a handsome garden, indicates his increasing prosperity. There his wife and children lived while he busied himself in the London theatres. The summer before he acquired New Place, his life was darkened by the death of his only son, Hamnet, a child of eleven. In May, 1602, Shakespeare purchased one hundred and seven acres of fertile farmland near Stratford and a few months later bought a cottage and garden across the alley from New Place. About 1611, he seems to have returned permanently to Stratford, for the next year a legal document refers to him as "William Shakespeare of Stratford-upon-Avon . . . gentleman." To achieve the desired appellation of gentleman, William Shakespeare had seen to it that the College of Heralds in 1596 granted his father a coat of arms. In one step he thus became a second-generation gentleman.

Shakespeare's daughter Susanna made a good match in 1607 with Dr. John Hall, a prominent and prosperous Stratford physician. His second daughter, Judith, did not marry until she was thirty-two years old, and then, under somewhat scandalous circumstances, she married Thomas Quiney, a Stratford vintner. On March 25, 1616, Shakespeare made his will, bequeathing his landed property to Susanna, £300 to Judith, certain sums to other relatives, and his second-best bed to his wife, Anne. Much has been made of the second-best bed, but the legacy probably indicates only that Anne liked that particular bed. Shakespeare, following the practice of the time, may have already arranged with Susanna for his wife's care. Finally, on April 23, 1616, the anniversary of his birth, William Shakespeare died, and he was buried on April 25 within the chancel of Trinity Church, as befitted an honored citizen. On

August 6, 1623, a few months before the publication of the collected edition of Shakespeare's plays, Anne Shakespeare joined her husband in death.

## THE PUBLICATION OF HIS PLAYS

During his lifetime Shakespeare made no effort to publish any of his plays, though eighteen appeared in print in single-play editions known as quartos. Some of these are corrupt versions known as "bad quartos." No quarto, so far as is known, had the author's approval. Plays were not considered "literature" any more than radio and television scripts today are considered literature. Dramatists sold their plays outright to the theatrical companies and it was usually considered in the company's interest to keep plays from getting into print. To achieve a reputation as a man of letters, Shakespeare wrote his *Sonnets* and his narrative poems, *Venus and Adonis* and *The Rape of Lucrece*, but he probably never dreamed that his plays would establish his reputation as a literary genius. Only Ben Jonson, a man known for his colossal conceit, had the crust to call his plays *Works*, as he did when he published an edition in 1616. But men laughed at Ben Jonson.

After Shakespeare's death, two of his old colleagues in the King's Men, John Heming and Henry Condell, decided that it would be a good thing to print, in more accurate versions than were then available, the plays already published and eighteen additional plays not previously published in quarto. In 1623 appeared *Mr. William Shakespeares Comedies, Histories, & Tragedies. Published according to the True Originall Copies. London. Printed by Isaac Iaggard and Ed. Blount.* This was the famous First Folio, a work that had the authority of Shakespeare's associates. The only play commonly attributed to Shakespeare that was omitted in the First Folio was *Pericles*. In their preface, "To the great Variety of Readers," Heming and Condell state that whereas "you were abused with diverse stolen and surreptitious copies, maimed and deformed by the frauds and stealths of injurious impostors that exposed them, even those are now offered to your view cured and perfect of their limbs; and all the rest, absolute in their numbers, as he conceived them." What they used for printer's copy is one of the vexed problems of scholarship, and skilled bibliographers have devoted years of study to the question of the relation of the "copy" for the First Folio to Shakespeare's manuscripts. In some cases it is clear that the editors corrected printed quarto versions of the plays, probably by comparison with playhouse scripts. Whether these scripts were in Shakespeare's autograph is anybody's guess. No manuscript of any play in Shakespeare's handwriting has survived. Indeed, very few play manuscripts from this period by any author are extant. The Tudor and Stuart periods had not yet learned to prize autographs and authors' original manuscripts.

Since the First Folio contains eighteen plays not previously printed, it is the only source for these. For the other eighteen, which had appeared in quarto versions, the First Folio also has the authority of an edition prepared and overseen by Shakespeare's colleagues and professional associates. But since editorial standards in 1623 were far from strict, and Heming and Condell were actors rather than editors by profession, the texts are sometimes careless. The printing and proofreading of the First Folio also left much to be desired, and some garbled passages have to be corrected and emended. The "good quarto" texts have to be taken into account in preparing a modern edition.

Because of the great popularity of Shakespeare through the centuries, the First Folio has become a prized book, but it is not a very rare one, for it is estimated that 238 copies are extant. The Folger Shakespeare Library in Washington, D.C., has seventy-nine copies of the First Folio, collected by the founder, Henry Clay Folger, who believed that a collation of as many texts as possible would reveal significant facts about the text of Shakespeare's plays. Dr. Charlton Hinman, using an ingenious machine of his own invention for mechanical collating, has made many discoveries that throw light on Shakespeare's text and on printing practices of the day.

The probability is that the First Folio of 1623 had an edition of between 1,000 and 1,250 copies. It is believed that it sold for £1, which made it an expensive book, for £1 in 1623 was equivalent to something between $40 and $50 in modern purchasing power.

During the seventeenth century, Shakespeare was sufficiently popular to warrant three later editions in folio size, the Second Folio of 1632, the Third Folio of 1663–1664, and the Fourth Folio of 1685. The Third Folio added six other plays ascribed to Shakespeare, but these are apocryphal.

## THE SHAKESPEAREAN THEATRE

The theatres in which Shakespeare's plays were performed were vastly different from those we know today.

The stage was a platform that jutted out into the area now occupied by the first rows of seats on the main floor, what is called the "orchestra" in America and the "pit" in England. This platform had no curtain to come down at the ends of acts and scenes. And although simple stage properties were available, the Elizabethan theatre lacked both the machinery and the elaborate movable scenery of the modern theatre. In the rear of the platform stage was a curtained area that could be used as an inner room, a tomb, or any such scene that might be required. A balcony above this inner room, and perhaps balconies on the sides of the stage, could represent the upper deck of a ship, the entry to Juliet's room, or a prison window. A trap door in the stage provided an entrance for ghosts and devils from the nether regions, and a similar trap in the canopied structure over the stage, known as the "heavens," made it possible to let down angels on a rope. These primitive stage arrangements help to account for many elements in Elizabethan plays. For example, since there was no curtain, the dramatist frequently felt the necessity of writing into his play action to clear the stage at the ends of acts and scenes. The funeral march at the end of *Hamlet* is not there merely for atmosphere; Shakespeare had to get the corpses off the stage. The lack of scenery also freed the dramatist from undue concern about the exact location of his sets, and the physical relation of his various settings to each other did not have to be worked out with the same precision as in the modern theatre.

Before London had buildings designed exclusively for theatrical entertainment, plays were given in inns and taverns. The characteristic inn of the period had an inner courtyard with rooms opening onto balconies overlooking the yard. Players could set up their temporary stages at one end of the yard and audiences could find seats on the balconies out of the weather. The poorer sort could stand or sit on the cobblestones in the yard, which was open to the sky. The first theatres followed this construction, and throughout the Elizabethan period the large public theatres had a yard in front of the stage open to the weather, with two or three tiers of covered balconies extending around the theatre. This physical structure again influenced the writing of plays. Because a dramatist wanted the actors to be heard, he frequently wrote into his play orations that could be delivered with declamatory effect. He also provided spectacle, buffoonery, and broad jests to keep the riotous groundlings in the yard entertained and quiet.

In another respect the Elizabethan theatre differed greatly from ours. It had no actresses. All women's roles were taken by boys, sometimes recruited from the boys' choirs of the London churches. Some of these youths acted their roles with great skill and the Elizabethans did not seem to be aware of any incongruity. The first actresses on the professional English stage appeared after the Restoration of Charles II, in 1660, when exiled Englishmen brought back from France practices of the French stage.

London in the Elizabethan period, as now, was the center of theatrical interest, though wandering actors from time to time traveled through the country performing in inns, halls, and the houses of the nobility. The first professional playhouse, called simply The Theatre, was erected by James Burbage, father of

Shakespeare's colleague Richard Burbage, in 1576 on lands of the old Holywell Priory adjacent to Finsbury Fields, a playground and park area just north of the city walls. It had the advantage of being outside the city's jurisdiction and yet was near enough to be easily accessible. Soon after The Theatre was opened, another playhouse called The Curtain was erected in the same neighborhood. Both of these playhouses had open courtyards and were probably polygonal in shape.

About the time The Curtain opened, Richard Farrant, Master of the Chapel Royal at Windsor and of St. Paul's, conceived the idea of opening a "private" theatre in the old monastery buildings of the Blackfriars, not far from St. Paul's Cathedral in the heart of the city. This theatre was ostensibly to train the choirboys in plays for presentation at Court. Actually, Farrant managed to present plays to paying audiences and achieved considerable success until aristocratic neighbors complained and had the theatres closed. This first Blackfriars Theatre was significant, however, because it popularized the boy actors in a professional way, and it paved the way for a second theatre in the Blackfriars, which Shakespeare's company took over more than thirty years later. By the last years of the sixteenth century, London had at least six professional theatres and still others were erected during the reign of James I.

The Globe Theatre, the playhouse that most people connect with Shakespeare, was erected early in 1599 on the Bankside, the area across the Thames from the city. Its construction had a dramatic beginning, for on the night of December 28, 1598, James Burbage's sons, Cuthbert and Richard, gathered together a crew who tore down the old theatre in Holywell and carted the

timbers across the river to a site that they had chosen
for a new playhouse. The reason for this clandestine
operation was a row with the landowner over the lease
to the Holywell property. The site chosen for the Globe
was another playground outside of the city's jurisdiction, a region of somewhat unsavory character. Not far
away was the Bear Garden, an amphitheatre devoted
to the baiting of bears and bulls. This was also the
region occupied by many houses of ill fame licensed by
the Bishop of Winchester and the source of substantial
revenue to him. But it was easily accessible either from
London Bridge or by means of the cheap boats operated
by the London watermen, and it had the great advantage of being beyond the authority of the Puritanical
aldermen of London, who frowned on plays because
they lured apprentices from work, filled their heads
with improper ideas, and generally exerted a bad influence. The aldermen also complained that the crowds
drawn together in the theatre helped to spread the
plague.

The Globe was the handsomest theatre up to its
time. It was a large octagonal building, open like its
predecessors to the sky in the center, but capable of
seating a large audience in its covered balconies. To
erect and operate the Globe, the Burbages organized
a syndicate composed of the leading members of the
dramatic company, of which Shakespeare was a member. Since it was open to the weather and depended on
natural light, plays had to be given in the afternoon.
This caused no hardship in the long afternoons of an
English summer, but in the winter the weather was a
great handicap and discouraged all except the hardiest.
For that reason, in 1608 Shakespeare's company was

glad to take over the lease of the second Blackfriars Theatre, a substantial, roomy hall reconstructed within the framework of the old monastery building. This theatre was protected from the weather and its stage was artificially lighted by chandeliers of candles. This became the winter playhouse for Shakespeare's company and at once proved so popular that the congestion of traffic created an embarrassing problem. Stringent regulations had to be made for the movement of coaches in the vicinity. Shakespeare's company continued to use the Globe during the summer months. In 1613 a squib fired from a cannon during a performance of *Henry VIII* fell on the thatched roof and the Globe burned to the ground. The next year it was rebuilt.

London had other famous theatres. The Rose, just west of the Globe, was built by Philip Henslowe, a semi-literate denizen of the Bankside, who became one of the most important theatrical owners and producers of the Tudor and Stuart periods. What is more important for historians, he kept a detailed account book, which provides much of our information about theatrical history in his time. Another famous theatre on the Bankside was the Swan, which a Dutch priest, Johannes de Witt, visited in 1596. The crude drawing of the stage which he made was copied by his friend Arend van Buchell; it is one of the important pieces of contemporary evidence for theatrical construction. De Witt described the Swan as capable of holding three thousand spectators. Among the other theatres, the Fortune, north of the city, on Golding Lane, and the Red Bull, even farther away from the city, off St. John's Street, were the most popular. The Red Bull, much frequented by apprentices, favored sensational and sometimes rowdy plays.

The actors who kept all of these theatres going were organized into companies under the protection of some noble patron. Traditionally actors had enjoyed a low reputation. In some of the ordinances they were classed as vagrants; in the phraseology of the time, "rogues, vagabonds, sturdy beggars, and common players" were all listed together as undesirables. To escape penalties often meted out to these characters, organized groups of actors managed to gain the protection of various personages of high degree. In the later years of Elizabeth's reign, a group flourished under the name of the Queen's Men; another group had the protection of the Lord Admiral and were known as the Lord Admiral's Men. Edward Alleyn, son-in-law of Philip Henslowe, was the leading spirit in the Lord Admiral's Men. Besides the adult companies, troupes of boy actors from time to time also enjoyed considerable popularity. Among these were the Children of Paul's and the Children of the Chapel Royal.

The company with which Shakespeare had a long association had for its patron Henry Carey, Lord Hunsdon, the Lord Chamberlain, and hence they were known as the Lord Chamberlain's Men. After the accession of James I, they became the King's Men. This company was the great rival of the Lord Admiral's Men, managed by Henslowe and Alleyn.

All was not easy for the players in Shakespeare's time, for the aldermen of London were always eager for an excuse to close up the Blackfriars and any other theatres in their jurisdiction. The theatres outside the jurisdiction of London were not immune from interference, for they might be shut up by order of the Privy Council for meddling in politics or for various other offenses, or they might be closed in time of plague, lest they spread infection. During plague times, the actors usually went on tour and played the provinces wherever they could find an audience. Particularly frightening were the plagues of 1592–1594 and 1613 when the theatres closed and the players, like many other Londoners, had to take to the country.

Though players had a low social status, they enjoyed great popularity, and one of the favorite forms of entertainment at Court was the performance of plays. To be commanded to perform at Court conferred great prestige upon a company of players, and printers frequently noted that fact when they published plays. Many of Shakespeare's plays were performed before the sovereign, and Shakespeare himself undoubtedly acted in some of these plays.

## REFERENCES FOR FURTHER READING

Many readers will want suggestions for further reading about Shakespeare and his times. The literature in this field is enormous but a few references will serve as guides to further study. A simple and useful little book is Gerald Sanders, *A Shakespeare Primer* (New York, 1950). *A Companion to Shakespeare Studies,* edited by Harley Granville-Barker and G. B. Harrison (Cambridge, Eng., 1934), is a valuable guide. More detailed but still not too voluminous to be confusing is Hazelton Spencer, *The Art and Life of William Shakespeare* (New York, 1940), which, like Sanders' handbook, contains a brief annotated list of useful books on various aspects of the subject. The most detailed and scholarly work providing complete factual information about Shakespeare is Sir Edmund Chambers, *William Shakespeare: A Study of Facts and Problems* (2 vols., Oxford, 1930). For detailed, factual information about the Elizabethan and seventeenth-century stages, the definitive reference works are Sir Edmund Chambers, *The Elizabethan Stage* (4 vols., Oxford, 1923) and Gerald E. Bentley, *The Jacobean and Caroline Stage* (5 vols., Oxford, 1941–1956). Alfred Harbage, *Shakespeare's Audience* (New York, 1941) throws light on the nature and tastes of the customers for whom Elizabethan dramatists wrote.

Although specialists disagree about details of stage construction, the reader will find essential information in John C. Adams, *The Globe Playhouse: Its Design and Equipment* (Barnes & Noble, 1961). A model of the Globe playhouse by Dr. Adams is on permanent exhibition in the Folger Shakespeare Library in Washington, D.C. An excellent description of the architecture of the Globe is Irwin Smith, *Shakespeare's Globe Playhouse: A Modern Reconstruction in Text and Scale Drawings Based upon the Reconstruction of the Globe by John Cranford Adams* (New York, 1956). An easily read history of the early theatres is J. Q. Adams, *Shakespearean Playhouses: A History of English Theatres from the Beginnings to the Restoration* (Boston, 1917).

The following titles on theatrical history will provide information about Shakespeare's plays in later periods: Alfred Harbage, *Theatre for Shakespeare* (Toronto, 1955); Esther Cloudman Dunn, *Shakespeare in America* (New York, 1939); George C. D. Odell, *Shakespeare from Betterton to Irving* (2 vols., London, 1921);

Arthur Colby Sprague, *Shakespeare and the Actors: The Stage Business in His Plays (1660–1905)* (Cambridge, Mass., 1944) and *Shakespearian Players and Performances* (Cambridge, Mass., 1953); Leslie Hotson, *The Commonwealth and Restoration Stage* (Cambridge, Mass., 1928); Alwin Thaler, *Shakspere to Sheridan: A Book About the Theatre of Yesterday and To-day* (Cambridge, Mass., 1922); Ernest Bradlee Watson, *Sheridan to Robertson: A Study of the 19th-Century London Stage* (Cambridge, Mass., 1926).

Harley Granville-Barker, *Prefaces to Shakespeare* (5 vols., London, 1927–1948) provides stimulating critical discussion of the plays. An older classic of criticism is Andrew C. Bradley, *Shakespearean Tragedy: Lectures on Hamlet, Othello, King Lear, Macbeth* (London, 1904), which is now available in an inexpensive reprint (New York, 1955). Thomas M. Parrott, *Shakespearean Comedy* (New York, 1949) is scholarly and readable. Shakespeare's dramatizations of English history are examined in E. M. W. Tillyard, *Shakespeare's History Plays* (London, 1948), and Lily Bess Campbell, *Shakespeare's "Histories," Mirrors of Elizabethan Policy* (San Marino, Calif., 1947) contains a more technical discussion of the same subject.

Interesting pictures as well as new information about Shakespeare will be found in F. E. Halliday, *Shakespeare, a Pictorial Biography* (London, 1956). Allardyce Nicoll, *The Elizabethans* (Cambridge, Eng., 1957) contains a variety of illustrations for the period.

Books discussing *Hamlet* are legion; few interpreters of the play agree with one another; and most are sharp controversialists. A highly controversial but stimulating example is J. Dover Wilson, *What Happens in Hamlet*

(3rd ed., Cambridge, Eng., 1951), which prompted a paper at a meeting of the Modern Language Association of America entitled "What Does Not Happen in *Hamlet.*" An interesting commentary on *Hamlet* is to be found in Joseph Q. Adams' edition of the play published by Houghton Mifflin in 1929. Stimulating and provocative is Miss Lily Bess Campbell's discussion in *Shakespeare's Tragic Heroes* (New York, 1930). Sensible and acute observations on *Hamlet* will be found in Miss Margaret Webster's *Shakespeare Without Tears* (New York, 1942).

A brief, clear, and accurate account of Tudor history is S. T. Bindoff, *The Tudors,* in the Penguin series. A readable general history is G. M. Trevelyan, *The History of England,* first published in 1926 and available in many editions. G. M. Trevelyan, *English Social History,* first published in 1942 and also available in many editions, provides fascinating information about England in all periods. Sir John Neale, *Queen Elizabeth* (London, 1934) is the best study of the great Queen. Various aspects of life in the Elizabethan period are treated in Louis B. Wright, *Middle-Class Culture in Elizabethan England* (Chapel Hill, N.C., 1935). *Shakespeare's England: An Account of the Life and Manners of His Age,* edited by Sidney Lee and C. T. Onions (2 vols., Oxford, 1916), provides a large amount of information on many aspects of life in the Elizabethan period. Additional information will be found in Muriel St. C. Byrne, *Elizabethan Life in Town and Country* (Barnes & Noble, 1961).

## [Dramatis Personae.

*Claudius*, King of Denmark.
*Hamlet*, nephew to the King.
*Polonius*, counselor to the King.
*Horatio*, friend to *Hamlet*.
*Laertes*, son to *Polonius*.
*Voltemand*,
*Cornelius*,
*Rosencrantz*,
*Guildenstern*, } courtiers.
*Osric*,
A gentleman,
*Marcellus*,
*Bernardo*, } soldiers.
*Francisco*,
*Reynaldo*, servant to *Polonius*.
*Fortinbras*, Prince of Norway.
Players.
Two Clowns, gravediggers.
A Norwegian Captain.
English Ambassadors.
*Gertrude*, Queen of Denmark, mother to *Hamlet*.
*Ophelia*, daughter to *Polonius*.
Ghost of Hamlet's Father.
Lords, Ladies, Priests, Officers, Soldiers, Sailors,
    Messengers, Attendants.

Scene: *Elsinore*.]

THE TRAGEDY OF

# HAMLET,

PRINCE OF DENMARK

ACT I

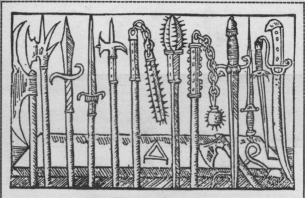

Weapons of war.
From Olaus Magnus, *Historia de gentibus septentrionalibus* (1555).

**I. i.** Horatio joins Marcellus and Bernardo on watch at the royal castle of Elsinore to confirm their reports of an apparition resembling the late King of Denmark. The specter appears but cannot be persuaded to speak before it vanishes at cockcrow. Horatio suggests that the dead King's son, Hamlet, be informed of this phenomenon, and the others agree that he may have more success in fathoming the purpose of the ghost's visitations.

▮▮▮▮▮▮▮▮▮▮▮▮▮▮▮▮▮▮▮▮▮▮▮▮▮▮▮▮▮

14. **rivals:** partners

# ACT I

||||||||||||||||||||||||||||||||||||||||||||||||||||||||||||||||||||||||||||||||||||||||||||||||||||||

Scene I. [Elsinore Castle. The platform of the watch.]
Enter *Bernardo* and *Francisco*, two sentinels [from
opposite directions].

*Ber.* Who's there?
*Fran.* Nay, answer me. Stand and unfold yourself.
*Ber.* Long live the King!
*Fran.* Bernardo?
*Ber.* He.                                                                    5
*Fran.* You come most carefully upon your hour.
*Ber.* 'Tis now struck twelve. Get thee to bed, Francisco.
*Fran.* For this relief much thanks. 'Tis bitter cold,
And I am sick at heart.
*Ber.* Have you had quiet guard?                        10
*Fran.*                                        Not a mouse stirring.
*Ber.* Well, good night.
If you do meet Horatio and Marcellus,
The rivals of my watch, bid them make haste.

Enter *Horatio* and *Marcellus*.

*Fran.* I think I hear them. Stand! Who's there?           15
*Hor.* Friends to this ground.

I

17. **Dane:** King of Denmark

26. **A piece of him:** a joke, reflecting Horatio's skepticism about the existence of ghosts; he is present but his heart is not in the venture.

30. **fantasy:** fancy

36. **approve our eyes:** corroborate what we have seen; **speak to it:** Horatio's friends believe that he, as a university student, will know how to address a spirit properly.

45. **the pole:** the North Pole

46. **his:** its; a common form

*Mar.*                    And liegemen to the Dane.
*Fran.* Give you good night.
*Mar.*                    O, farewell, honest soldier.
Who hath relieved you?                                        20
*Fran.*          Bernardo hath my place.
Give you good night.                              *Exit.*
*Mar.*          Holla, Bernardo!
*Ber.*                    Say—
What, is Horatio there?                                       25
*Hor.*               A piece of him.
*Ber.* Welcome, Horatio. Welcome, good Marcellus.
*Mar.* What, has this thing appeared again tonight?
*Ber.* I have seen nothing.
*Mar.* Horatio says 'tis but our fantasy,                     30
And will not let belief take hold of him
Touching this dreaded sight, twice seen of us.
Therefore I have entreated him along,
With us to watch the minutes of this night,
That, if again this apparition come,                          35
He may approve our eyes and speak to it.
*Hor.* Tush, tush, 'twill not appear.
*Ber.*                    Sit down awhile,
And let us once again assail your ears,
That are so fortified against our story,                      40
What we two nights have seen.
*Hor.*               Well, sit we down,
And let us hear Bernardo speak of this.
*Ber.* Last night of all,
When yond same star that's westward from the pole            45
Had made his course t' illume that part of heaven
Where now it burns, Marcellus and myself,
The bell then beating one—

58. **buried Denmark:** the dead king of Denmark
66. **on't:** of it
67. **might:** could
68-9. **the sensible and true avouch/ Of mine own eyes:** the evidence of my own eyes, based on the senses and therefore believable
73. **Norway:** ruler of Norway, Fortinbras senior
74. **parle:** parley
75. **sledded Polacks:** that is, Polish soldiers in sleds. Textual scholars have long debated this passage. The early editions of the play printed the word "pollax" and some editors have held that it should be "poleax." Edmund Malone was the first to emend it to "Polacks."

Personal combat.
From Olaus Magnus, *Historia de gentibus septentrionalibus* (1555).

3

Enter *Ghost*.

*Mar.* Peace! break thee off! Look where it comes again!
*Ber.* In the same figure, like the King that's dead.                    50
*Mar.* Thou art a scholar; speak to it, Horatio.
*Ber.* Looks it not like the King? Mark it, Horatio.
*Hor.* Most like. It harrows me with fear and wonder.
*Ber.* It would be spoke to.
*Mar.*                          Question it, Horatio.                    55
*Hor.* What art thou that usurp'st this time of night
Together with that fair and warlike form
In which the majesty of buried Denmark
Did sometimes march? By heaven I charge thee speak!
*Mar.* It is offended.                                                  60
*Ber.*                          See, it stalks away!
*Hor.* Stay! Speak, speak! I charge thee speak!

                                              *Exit Ghost.*

*Mar.* 'Tis gone and will not answer.
*Ber.* How now, Horatio? You tremble and look pale.
Is not this something more than fantasy?                                65
What think you on't?
*Hor.* Before my God, I might not this believe
Without the sensible and true avouch
Of mine own eyes.
*Mar.*              Is it not like the King?                            70
*Hor.* As thou art to thyself.
Such was the very armor he had on
When he the ambitious Norway combated;
So frowned he once when, in an angry parle,
He smote the sledded Polacks on the ice.                               75
'Tis strange.

77. **jump:** exactly

79-80: **In what particular thought to work I know not;/ But, in the gross and scope of my opinion:** I do not know exactly what to think but my general opinion is that

82. **Good now:** a courteous expression, "if you please"

84. **toils the subject of the land:** wearies the Danish subjects

86. **foreign mart:** trade abroad

87. **impress:** conscription

89. **might be toward:** could be in the offing

96. **emulate:** envious

99. **by a sealed compact:** in accordance with terms agreed upon

100. **by law and heraldry:** heraldic law; that is, the law decreed by the heralds of Denmark and Norway to govern the combat

102. **stood seized of:** owned

103. **a moiety competent:** an adequate portion

104. **gaged:** pledged; **had:** would have

106. **comart:** agreement

107. **carriage of the article designed:** tenor of the stipulation on the point

*Mar.* Thus twice before, and jump at this dead hour,
With martial stalk hath he gone by our watch.

*Hor.* In what particular thought to work I know not;
But, in the gross and scope of my opinion,                    80
This bodes some strange eruption to our state.

*Mar.* Good now, sit down, and tell me he that knows,
Why this same strict and most observant watch
So nightly toils the subject of the land,
And why such daily cast of brazen cannon                      85
And foreign mart for implements of war;
Why such impress of shipwrights, whose sore task
Does not divide the Sunday from the week;
What might be toward, that this sweaty haste
Doth make the night joint-laborer with the day?               90
Who is't that can inform me?

*Hor.*                         That can I.
At least, the whisper goes so. Our last King,
Whose image even but now appeared to us,
Was, as you know, by Fortinbras of Norway,                    95
Thereto pricked on by a most emulate pride,
Dared to the combat; in which our valiant Hamlet
(For so this side of our known world esteemed him)
Did slay this Fortinbras; who, by a sealed compact,
Well ratified by law and heraldry,                            100
Did forfeit, with his life, all those his lands
Which he stood seized of, to the conqueror;
Against the which a moiety competent
Was gaged by our King; which had returned
To the inheritance of Fortinbras,                             105
Had he been vanquisher, as, by the same comart
And carriage of the article designed,

109. **unimproved:** that is, not otherwise profitably occupied; **mettle:** courage

111. **Sharked up a list:** gathered voraciously, enlisted. **List** also meant "selvage," which would carry out the imagery of **skirts** in l. 110; **resolutes:** adventurers, desperadoes

112. **For food and diet:** as cannon fodder

113. **hath a stomach in't:** requires courage

114. **state:** government

119. **head:** source

120. **post-haste:** a superscription urging speedy delivery of mail, indicating, as used here, frantic speed in the military preparation they are discussing; **romage:** bustle, commotion

121. **it be no other but e'en so:** it is exactly so.

122. **Well may it sort:** it may well be appropriate.

124. **question:** subject of controversy

126. **palmy:** flourishing

128-33. Shakespeare is enumerating a list of prodigies seen in Rome before Caesar's death.

130. **As stars with trains of fire:** The construction here is awkward, since **As** refers to nothing. A preceding line may have been omitted by the printer in error. The whole passage is omitted from the Folio text. **Stars with trains of fire** are meteors.

131. **Disasters in the sun:** signs of disaster exhibited by the sun; **the moist star:** the moon

132. **Upon whose influence Neptune's empire stands:** a reference to the moon's control of the tides. Neptune was the ancient Italian god of the sea.

133, 134, 135, 136: see next page.     **5**

His fell to Hamlet. Now, sir, young Fortinbras,
Of unimproved mettle hot and full,
Hath in the skirts of Norway, here and there, 110
Sharked up a list of lawless resolutes,
For food and diet to some enterprise
That hath a stomach in't; which is no other,
As it doth well appear unto our state,
But to recover of us, by strong hand 115
And terms compulsatory, those foresaid lands
So by his father lost; and this, I take it,
Is the main motive of our preparations,
The source of this our watch, and the chief head
Of this post-haste and romage in the land. 120
  *Ber.* I think it be no other but e'en so.
Well may it sort that this portentous figure
Comes armed through our watch, so like the King
That was and is the question of these wars.
  *Hor.* A mote it is to trouble the mind's eye. 125
In the most high and palmy state of Rome,
A little ere the mightiest Julius fell,
The graves stood tenantless, and the sheeted dead
Did squeak and gibber in the Roman streets;
As stars with trains of fire, and dews of blood, 130
Disasters in the sun; and the moist star
Upon whose influence Neptune's empire stands
Was sick almost to doomsday with eclipse.
And even the like precurse of fierce events,
As harbingers preceding still the fates 135
And prologue to the omen coming on,
Have heaven and earth together demonstrated
Unto our climatures and countrymen.

133. **sick almost to doomsday with eclipse:** a reference to the Biblical promise of a lightless moon on the Day of Judgment (Matthew 24:29)

134. **even the like:** exactly the same; **precurse:** precursor, forerunner

135. **harbingers:** similar in sense to **precurse.** A **harbinger** was a servant or officer who preceded his superiors to arrange for accommodations; **still:** always; **the fates:** personified in classical mythology as three women

136. **omen:** that is, the portended calamity itself; **coming on:** approaching

139. **soft:** hold.

140. **cross it: cross** has a double meaning here, "intercept" and "make the sign of the cross to avert evil."

144. **to thee do ease:** ease you; **grace to me:** bring me credit

146. **privy to:** informed of

147. **happily:** haply, perhaps

153. **partisan:** long-handled weapon, like a pike

161. **malicious mockery:** mock malice only, because ineffectual

Enter *Ghost* again.

But soft! behold! Lo, where it comes again!
I'll cross it, though it blast me.—Stay, illusion! 140
If thou hast any sound, or use of voice,
Speak to me.
If there be any good thing to be done,
That may to thee do ease, and grace to me,
Speak to me. 145
If thou art privy to thy country's fate,
Which happily foreknowing may avoid,
O, speak!
Or if thou hast uphoarded in thy life
Extorted treasure in the womb of earth 150
(For which, they say, you spirits oft walk in death),
*The cock crows.*
Speak of it! Stay, and speak!—Stop it, Marcellus!
 *Mar.* Shall I strike at it with my partisan?
 *Hor.* Do, if it will not stand.
 *Ber.*                    'Tis here! 155
 *Hor.*                         'Tis here!
 *Mar.* 'Tis gone!
                    *Exit Ghost.*
We do it wrong, being so majestical,
To offer it the show of violence;
For it is as the air, invulnerable, 160
And our vain blows malicious mockery.
 *Ber.* It was about to speak, when the cock crew.
 *Hor.* And then it started, like a guilty thing
Upon a fearful summons. I have heard
The cock, that is the trumpet to the morn, 165

169. **extravagant and erring**: both synonyms for "straying," "wandering from normal limits"; **hies**: hurries

171. **made probation**: proved

173. **'gainst**: just before

177. **strike**: blast with misfortune. Belief in the evil influence which the planets could exert was common.

178. **takes**: bewitches

181. **russet**: formerly the name of a rough homespun used for the clothing of country folk, and ranging in color from reddish-brown to gray

188. **needful in our loves, fitting our duty**: necessary and dutiful behavior as his friends

Doth with his lofty and shrill-sounding throat
Awake the god of day; and at his warning,
Whether in sea or fire, in earth or air,
The extravagant and erring spirit hies
To his confine; and of the truth herein                    170
This present object made probation.

   *Mar.* It faded on the crowing of the cock.
Some say that ever 'gainst that season comes
Wherein our Saviour's birth is celebrated,
The bird of dawning singeth all night long;                 175
And then, they say, no spirit dare stir abroad,
The nights are wholesome, then no planets strike,
No fairy takes, nor witch hath power to charm,
So hallowed and so gracious is the time.

   *Hor.* So have I heard and do in part believe it.   180
But look, the morn, in russet mantle clad,
Walks o'er the dew of yon high eastern hill.
Break we our watch up; and by my advice
Let us impart what we have seen tonight
Unto young Hamlet; for, upon my life,                       185
This spirit, dumb to us, will speak to him.
Do you consent we shall acquaint him with it,
As needful in our loves, fitting our duty?

   *Mar.* Let's do't, I pray; and I this morning know
Where we shall find him most conveniently.                  190

                                       *Exeunt.*

**I. ii.** Claudius, King of Denmark, expresses his thanks to his subjects and attendants for their assistance in the ceremonies at his brother's funeral and his own marriage to his brother's wife, Gertrude. He sends ambassadors to the King of Norway to urge him to curb the activities of his nephew Fortinbras, who is threatening invasion to recover lands lost by his father. Laertes, son of Claudius' chief counselor, Polonius, is given permission to return to France. Aside, Hamlet, the grieving son of the late King, reveals his disillusionment and disgust at his mother's speedy marriage to his uncle.

Horatio, Marcellus, and Bernardo tell Hamlet of the ghost. He hears their story with alarmed interest and agrees to join their watch that night.

▬▬▬▬▬▬▬▬▬▬▬▬▬▬▬

8. **sometime:** erstwhile, former

9. **jointress:** a widow who has inherited property rights, provided in a "jointure," to be shared

10. **defeated:** overcome

11. **With an auspicious, and a dropping eye:** that is, half-joyfully, half-tearfully

13. **dole:** grief

17. **that:** what

18. **a weak supposal of our worth:** a poor estimation of my ability

21. **Colleagued:** allied; **advantage:** superiority

22. **pester us with message:** bother me with frequent messages. **Pester** meant to annoy and also carried the sense of crowding.

24. **bands of law:** legal bonds

Scene II. [Elsinore Castle. An audience chamber.]

*Flourish.* Enter *Claudius, King of Denmark, Gertrude the
Queen, Hamlet, Polonius, Laertes* and his sister *Ophelia,
Lords Attendant.*

*King.* Though yet of Hamlet our dear brother's death
The memory be green, and that it us befitted
To bear our hearts in grief, and our whole kingdom
To be contracted in one brow of woe,
Yet so far hath discretion fought with nature                    5
That we with wisest sorrow think on him
Together with remembrance of ourselves.
Therefore our sometime sister, now our queen,
The imperial jointress to this warlike state,
Have we, as 'twere with a defeated joy,                          10
With an auspicious, and a dropping eye,
With mirth in funeral, and with dirge in marriage,
In equal scale weighing delight and dole,
Taken to wife; nor have we herein barred
Your better wisdoms, which have freely gone                      15
With this affair along. For all, our thanks.
Now follows, that you know, young Fortinbras,
Holding a weak supposal of our worth,
Or thinking by our late dear brother's death
Our state to be disjoint and out of frame,                       20
Colleagued with this dream of his advantage,
He hath not failed to pester us with message
Importing the surrender of those lands
Lost by his father, with all bands of law,
To our most valiant brother. So much for him.                    25

Fighting Norsemen.
From Olaus Magnus, *Historia de gentibus septentrionalibus* (1555).

31. **His further gait herein:** his proceeding in this affair; **in that:** on the basis of the fact that

37. **To business:** to do business

38. **dilated articles:** detailed account of the situation

39. **let your haste commend your duty:** show your duty in a speedy departure rather than ceremonious farewells.

45. **Dane:** King of Denmark, as in I. i. 17

48. **native:** naturally related

53. **leave and favor:** favorable leave, permission

9

Enter *Voltemand* and *Cornelius*.

Now for ourself and for this time of meeting.
Thus much the business is: we have here writ
To Norway, uncle of young Fortinbras,
Who, impotent and bedrid, scarcely hears
Of this his nephew's purpose, to suppress                    30
His further gait herein, in that the levies,
The lists, and full proportions are all made
Out of his subject; and we here dispatch
You, good Cornelius, and you, Voltemand,
For bearers of this greeting to old Norway,                  35
Giving to you no further personal power
To business with the King, more than the scope
Of these dilated articles allow.          [*Gives a paper.*]
Farewell, and let your haste commend your duty.
   *Cor., Volt.* In that, and all things, will we show our   40
    duty.
   *King.* We doubt it nothing. Heartily farewell.
                *Exeunt Voltemand and Cornelius.*
And now, Laertes, what's the news with you?
You told us of some suit. What is't, Laertes?
You cannot speak of reason to the Dane                       45
And lose your voice. What wouldst thou beg, Laertes,
That shall not be my offer, not thy asking?
The head is not more native to the heart,
The hand more instrumental to the mouth,
Than is the throne of Denmark to thy father.                 50
What wouldst thou have, Laertes?
   *Laer.*                        My dread lord,
Your leave and favor to return to France,

65. **Take thy fair hour:** make the most of your youth; "gather ye rosebuds while ye may."

66. **thy best graces spend it at thy will:** may your virtues control the way in which you spend it.

67. **cousin:** kinsman; actually, Hamlet is his nephew.

68-9. **A little more than kin, and less than kind:** Hamlet is ironic and mutters that he and his uncle are more than kin (twice related: uncle/nephew and stepfather/stepson) but they are not kindred spirits.

71. **i' the sun:** a pun on sun/son, betraying Hamlet's resentment at his new relationship with Claudius

72. **nighted:** dark

74. **vailed:** lowered, downcast

76. **common:** common to every mortal; universal

80. **Why seems it so particular with thee:** why do you take it so personally to heart as though your loss were unique.

85. **fruitful:** abundant

From whence though willingly I came to Denmark
To show my duty in your coronation,                     55
Yet now I must confess, that duty done,
My thoughts and wishes bend again toward France
And bow them to your gracious leave and pardon.
    *King.* Have you your father's leave? What says Polo-
      nius?                                              60
    *Pol.* He hath, my lord, wrung from me my slow leave
By laborsome petition, and at last
Upon his will I sealed my hard consent.
I do beseech you give him leave to go.
    *King.* Take thy fair hour, Laertes. Time be thine,   65
And thy best graces spend it at thy will!
But now, my cousin Hamlet, and my son—
    *Ham.* [*Aside*] A little more than kin, and less than
      kind!
    *King.* How is it that the clouds still hang on you?    70
    *Ham.* Not so, my lord. I am too much i' the sun.
    *Queen.* Good Hamlet, cast thy nighted color off,
And let thine eye look like a friend on Denmark.
Do not for ever with thy vailed lids
Seek for thy noble father in the dust.                   75
Thou know'st 'tis common, all that lives must die,
Passing through nature to eternity.
    *Ham.* Ay, madam, it is common.
    *Queen.*                          If it be,
Why seems it so particular with thee?                    80
    *Ham.* Seems, madam? Nay, it is. I know not "seems."
'Tis not alone my inky cloak, good mother,
Nor customary suits of solemn black,
Nor windy suspiration of forced breath,
No, nor the fruitful river in the eye,                   85

A warrior's funeral.
From Olaus Magnus, *Historia de gentibus septentrionalibus* (1555).

86. **havior:** behavior
98. **To do obsequious sorrow:** demonstrate sorrow suitable for a funeral; **persever:** persevere
99. **obstinate condolement:** persistent need of consolation
101. **incorrect to heaven:** unresponsive to the divine will
105. **most vulgar thing to sense:** most familiar object of sensible perception
106. **peevish:** childish
110. **still:** always, habitually; see I. i. 135.
111. **corse:** corpse
113. **unprevailing:** vain

Nor the dejected havior of the visage,
Together with all forms, moods, shapes of grief,
That can denote me truly. These indeed seem,
For they are actions that a man might play;
But I have that within which passeth show—                    90
These but the trappings and the suits of woe.
   *King.* 'Tis sweet and commendable in your nature,
     Hamlet,
To give these mourning duties to your father;
But you must know, your father lost a father;                    95
That father lost, lost his, and the survivor bound
In filial obligation for some term
To do obsequious sorrow. But to persever
In obstinate condolement is a course
Of impious stubbornness. 'Tis unmanly grief;                    100
It shows a will most incorrect to heaven,
A heart unfortified, a mind impatient,
An understanding simple and unschooled;
For what we know must be, and is as common
As any the most vulgar thing to sense,                    105
Why should we in our peevish opposition
Take it to heart? Fie! 'tis a fault to heaven,
A fault against the dead, a fault to nature,
To reason most absurd, whose common theme
Is death of fathers, and who still hath cried,                    110
From the first corse till he that died today,
"This must be so." We pray you throw to earth
This unprevailing woe, and think of us
As of a father; for let the world take note
You are the most immediate to our throne,                    115
And with no less nobility of love
Than that which dearest father bears his son

118. **impart toward you:** express myself to you

120. **retrograde:** opposed, contrary

121. **bend you:** submit your will

128. **Be as ourself:** behave with all the freedom of the King himself.

130. **in grace whereof:** in honor of which

133. **rouse:** deep draught of liquor, carousal; **bruit:** report

135. **solid:** some modern bibliographers argue a case for "sallied" (a variant form of "sullied"), which appears in the First and Second Quartos. They insist that this word emphasizes Hamlet's feeling of personal defilement from his mother's incestuous marriage. However, **solid,** of the First Folio, introduces a more forceful metaphor, and Hamlet's disgust at his mother's incest is made explicit elsewhere in the soliloquy. Margaret Webster comments in *Shakespeare Without Tears* that for stage purposes the reading *solid* is preferable because it is imbedded in tradition. Certain editors, Miss Webster observes, "support with passion" the reading *sullied,* but she adds, "I cannot myself see quite why they are so greatly disturbed by *solid.*" We have retained **solid** because there seems no valid reason to reject the Folio reading, which has been traditionally preferred.

146. **Hyperion to a satyr:** the Greek god of the sun, of ideal manly beauty, was sometimes known as Hyperion. A satyr was a spirit, manlike in form, but with goatlike ears and tail.

147. **might not beteem:** could not permit

Do I impart toward you. For your intent
In going back to school in Wittenberg,
It is most retrograde to our desire;                    120
And we beseech you, bend you to remain
Here in the cheer and comfort of our eye,
Our chiefest courtier, cousin, and our son.
    *Queen.* Let not thy mother lose her prayers, Hamlet:
I pray thee stay with us, go not to Wittenberg.          125
    *Ham.* I shall in all my best obey you, madam.
    *King.* Why, 'tis a loving and a fair reply.
Be as ourself in Denmark. Madam, come.
This gentle and unforced accord of Hamlet
Sits smiling to my heart; in grace whereof,             130
No jocund health that Denmark drinks today
But the great cannon to the clouds shall tell,
And the King's rouse the heaven shall bruit again,
Respeaking earthly thunder. Come away.
                    *Flourish. Exeunt all but Hamlet.*
    *Ham.* O that this too too solid flesh would melt,   135
Thaw, and resolve itself into a dew!
Or that the Everlasting had not fixed
His canon 'gainst self-slaughter! O God! God!
How weary, stale, flat, and unprofitable
Seem to me all the uses of this world!                  140
Fie on't! ah, fie! 'Tis an unweeded garden
That grows to seed; things rank and gross in nature
Possess it merely. That it should come to this!
But two months dead—nay, not so much, not two!
So excellent a king, that was to this                   145
Hyperion to a satyr; so loving to my mother
That he might not beteem the winds of heaven
Visit her face too roughly. Heaven and earth!

153. **or ere:** before

155. **Niobe:** a proud woman in Greek mythology, who offended the goddess Leto and was punished by the death of her children and her own transformation to a stone which appeared to weep continually

156. **wants:** lacks; **discourse of reason:** the ability to reason, rationality

159. **Hercules:** the superman of classical mythology

160. **unrighteous:** not pure and virtuous, because they were insincere

161. **flushing:** inflammation; **galled:** irritated

163. **incestuous:** according to contemporary theology, the marriage of a woman with her husband's brother was incestuous.

170-71. **I'll change that name with you:** that is, I would have us call each other "friend"—no more talk of servants.

172. **what make you:** what are you doing.

Must I remember? Why, she would hang on him
As if increase of appetite had grown                              150
By what it fed on; and yet, within a month—
Let me not think on't! Frailty, thy name is woman!—
A little month, or ere those shoes were old
With which she followed my poor father's body
Like Niobe, all tears—why she, even she                          155
(O God! a beast that wants discourse of reason
Would have mourned longer) married with my uncle;
My father's brother, but no more like my father
Than I to Hercules. Within a month,
Ere yet the salt of most unrighteous tears                       160
Had left the flushing in her galled eyes,
She married. O, most wicked speed, to post
With such dexterity to incestuous sheets!
It is not, nor it cannot come to good.
But break my heart, for I must hold my tongue!                   165

Enter *Horatio, Marcellus,* and *Bernardo.*

*Hor.* Hail to your lordship!
*Ham.*                           I am glad to see you well.
Horatio—or I do forget myself!
*Hor.* The same, my lord, and your poor servant ever.
*Ham.* Sir, my good friend—I'll change that name with    170
    you.
And what make you from Wittenberg, Horatio?
Marcellus?
*Mar.* My good lord!
*Ham.* I am very glad to see you.—[*To Bernardo*] Good    175
    even, sir.—
But what, in faith, make you from Wittenberg?

A satyr.

From Vincenzo Cartari, *Imagini delli Dei de gl'Antichi* (1674).
(See I. ii. 146.)

188. **hard upon:** soon after

189. **funeral baked meats:** meat pies, which were served at the funeral feast

190. **coldly:** as cold leftovers

191. **dearest:** bitterest, most hated. "Dear" was used to express intensity of feeling.

203. **Season your admiration:** moderate your wonder.

*14*

*Hor.* A truant disposition, good my lord.

*Ham.* I would not hear your enemy say so,
Nor shall you do my ear that violence                    180
To make it truster of your own report
Against yourself. I know you are no truant.
But what is your affair in Elsinore?
We'll teach you to drink deep ere you depart.

*Hor.* My lord, I came to see your father's funeral.    185

*Ham.* I prithee do not mock me, fellow student,
I think it was to see my mother's wedding.

*Hor.* Indeed, my lord, it followed hard upon.

*Ham.* Thrift, thrift, Horatio! The funeral baked meats
Did coldly furnish forth the marriage tables.           190
Would I had met my dearest foe in heaven
Or ever I had seen that day, Horatio!
My father—methinks I see my father.

*Hor.* O, where, my lord?

*Ham.*                      In my mind's eye, Horatio.    195

*Hor.* I saw him once. He was a goodly king.

*Ham.* He was a man, take him for all in all.
I shall not look upon his like again.

*Hor.* My lord, I think I saw him yesternight.

*Ham.* Saw? who?                                        200

*Hor.* My lord, the King your father.

*Ham.*                              The King my father?

*Hor.* Season your admiration for a while
With an attent ear, till I may deliver,
Upon the witness of these gentlemen,                    205
This marvel to you.

*Ham.*              For God's love let me hear!

*Hor.* Two nights together had these gentlemen
(Marcellus and Bernardo) on their watch

210. **dead vast**: illimitable darkness. Both the First Folio and the Second Quarto read "waste." "Vast" is the reading of the First Quarto.

212. **at point**: at every point, fully; **cap-a-pe**: from head to foot

215. **oppressed and fear-surprised eyes**: both adjectives have a similar sense and describe the stupefied fright provoked in the two witnesses. **Oppressed** here means "taken by surprise."

216. **truncheon**: short staff, a symbol of authority which the elder Hamlet as King would have carried when armed for combat

217. **with the act of fear**: by the action of fear upon them

230. **it head**: its head. **It** was one form of the genitive more often expressed as "his."

232. **even**: just

In the dead vast and middle of the night                          210
Been thus encount'red. A figure like your father,
Armed at point exactly, cap-a-pe,
Appears before them and with solemn march
Goes slow and stately by them. Thrice he walked
By their oppressed and fear-surprised eyes,                        215
Within his truncheon's length; whilst they, distilled
Almost to jelly with the act of fear,
Stand dumb and speak not to him. This to me
In dreadful secrecy impart they did,
And I with them the third night kept the watch;                   220
Where, as they had delivered, both in time,
Form of the thing, each word made true and good,
The apparition comes. I knew your father:
These hands are not more like.
    *Ham.*               But where was this?     225
    *Mar.* My lord, upon the platform where we watched.
    *Ham.* Did you not speak to it?
    *Hor.*             My lord, I did;
But answer made it none. Yet once methought
It lifted up it head and did address                              230
Itself to motion, like as it would speak;
But even then the morning cock crew loud,
And at the sound it shrunk in haste away
And vanished from our sight.
    *Ham.*           'Tis very strange.     235
    *Hor.* As I do live, my honored lord, 'tis true;
And we did think it writ down in our duty
To let you know of it.
    *Ham.* Indeed, indeed, sirs, but this troubles me.
Hold you the watch tonight?                                       240
    *Both* [*Mar. and Ber.*]    We do, my lord.

Men-at-arms.
From Olaus Magnus, *Historia de gentibus septentrionalibus* (1555).

247. **beaver:** visor of his armor
256. **Very like:** most likely
261. **grizzled:** gray; with gray mingled in it
268. **hell itself should gape:** Hamlet refers to the possibility that the apparition is a demon instead of the spirit of his father.
271. **tenable:** held

*Ham.* Armed, say you?

*Both.* Armed, my lord.

*Ham.* From top to toe?

*Both.*            My lord, from head to foot.   245

*Ham.* Then saw you not his face?

*Hor.* O, yes, my lord! He wore his beaver up.

*Ham.* What, looked he frowningly?

*Hor.* A countenance more in sorrow than in anger.

*Ham.* Pale or red?           250

*Hor.* Nay, very pale.

*Ham.*           And fixed his eyes upon you?

*Hor.* Most constantly.

*Ham.*           I would I had been there.

*Hor.* It would have much amazed you.   255

*Ham.* Very like, very like. Stayed it long?

*Hor.* While one with moderate haste might tell a hundred.

*Both.* Longer, longer.

*Hor.* Not when I saw't.           260

*Ham.*           His beard was grizzled—no?

*Hor.* It was, as I have seen it in his life,
A sable silvered.

*Ham.*       I will watch tonight.
Perchance 'twill walk again.           265

*Hor.*           I warr'nt it will.

*Ham.* If it assume my noble father's person,
I'll speak to it, though hell itself should gape
And bid me hold my peace. I pray you all,
If you have hitherto concealed this sight,   270
Let it be tenable in your silence still;
And whatsoever else shall hap tonight,
Give it an understanding but no tongue.

**278. Your loves, as mine to you:** as before, Hamlet indicates his preference for friendship instead of dutiful behavior.

**280. doubt:** suspect

▌▌▌▌▌▌▌▌▌▌▌▌▌▌▌▌▌▌▌▌▌▌▌▌▌▌▌▌▌▌▌▌▌▌▌▌▌▌▌

**I. iii.** Laertes bids farewell to his sister, Ophelia, and warns her to be wary of taking Hamlet's attentions too seriously. Polonius enters and echoes Laertes' warnings emphatically. Though Ophelia protests that Hamlet's love is honorable and sincere, Polonius discounts her judgment and orders her to refuse to see him thereafter. Ophelia meekly submits.

▌▌▌▌▌▌▌▌▌▌▌▌▌▌▌▌▌▌▌▌▌▌▌▌▌▌▌▌▌▌▌▌

**2-4. as the winds give benefit/ And convoy is assistant . . . / . . . let me hear from you:** take advantage of favorable winds and convenient convoys to write me regularly.

**7. a fashion, and a toy in blood:** a fad, and a whim of his youthful amorousness

**8. the youth of primy nature:** the early spring of life. **Primy** means "of the springtime."

**9. Forward:** early, precocious

**10. suppliance:** supply; that is, pastime

**12. No more but so:** nothing more than that

**14. nature:** that is, the nature of a human being; **crescent:** growing

I will requite your loves. So, fare you well.
Upon the platform, 'twixt eleven and twelve,              275
I'll visit you.
    *All.*       Our duty to your honor.
    *Ham.* Your loves, as mine to you. Farewell.
                   *Exeunt [all but Hamlet].*
My father's spirit—in arms? All is not well.
I doubt some foul play. Would the night were come!         280
Till then sit still, my soul. Foul deeds will rise,
Though all the earth o'erwhelm them, to men's eyes.
                            *Exit.*

Scene III. [Elsinore. *Polonius'* house.]

Enter *Laertes* and *Ophelia.*

    *Laer.* My necessaries are embarked. Farewell.
And, sister, as the winds give benefit
And convoy is assistant, do not sleep,
But let me hear from you.
    *Oph.*          Do you doubt that?            5
    *Laer.* For Hamlet, and the trifling of his favor,
Hold it a fashion, and a toy in blood;
A violet in the youth of primy nature,
Forward, not permanent—sweet, not lasting;
The perfume and suppliance of a minute;                    10
No more.
    *Oph.* No more but so?
    *Laer.*          Think it no more.
For nature crescent does not grow alone

15. **thews**: bodily strength; **this temple waxes**: this body grows.

17. **withal**: at the same time

18. **cautel**: deceit

20. **His greatness weighed**: if his noble birth is considered

23. **Carve for himself**: follow his own inclination

26. **that body**: that is, the Danish state

30. **give his saying deed**: act upon his words of love

33. **credent**: believing; **list**: listen to

37. **keep you in the rear of your affection**: hold yourself back from the impetuous action your emotions might lead you to.

39. **chariest**: most reserved

42. **canker galls**: cankerworm damages; **the infants of the spring**: the earliest spring blossoms

43. **buttons**: buds

In thews and bulk, but as this temple waxes, 15
The inward service of the mind and soul
Grows wide withal. Perhaps he loves you now,
And now no soil nor cautel doth besmirch
The virtue of his will; but you must fear,
His greatness weighed, his will is not his own, 20
For he himself is subject to his birth.
He may not, as unvalued persons do,
Carve for himself, for on his choice depends
The safety and health of his whole state,
And therefore must his choice be circumscribed 25
Unto the voice and yielding of that body
Whereof he is the head. Then if he says he loves you,
It fits your wisdom so far to believe it
As he in his particular act and place
May give his saying deed, which is no further 30
Than the main voice of Denmark goes withal.
Then weigh what loss your honor may sustain
If with too credent ear you list his songs,
Or lose your heart, or your chaste treasure open
To his unmast'red importunity. 35
Fear it, Ophelia, fear it, my dear sister,
And keep you in the rear of your affection,
Out of the shot and danger of desire.
The chariest maid is prodigal enough
If she unmask her beauty to the moon. 40
Virtue itself scapes not calumnious strokes.
The canker galls the infants of the spring
Too oft before their buttons be disclosed,
And in the morn and liquid dew of youth
Contagious blastments are most imminent. 45

47. **Youth to itself rebels, though none else near:** with the least temptation, youth is liable to violate its better nature.

50. **ungracious:** ungodly

54. **recks:** heeds; **rede:** counsel

58. **Occasion smiles upon a second leave:** a favorable opportunity is offered for a second farewell.

61. **stayed:** waited

63. **Look thou character:** see that you inscribe

64. **unproportioned:** undisciplined, unreasonable

65. **vulgar:** common, too readily accessible to any friendship

73. **censure:** synonymous with **judgment**

Be wary then; best safety lies in fear.
Youth to itself rebels, though none else near.
    *Oph.* I shall the effect of this good lesson keep
As watchman to my heart. But, good my brother,
Do not as some ungracious pastors do,                          50
Show me the steep and thorny way to heaven,
Whiles, like a puffed and reckless libertine,
Himself the primrose path of dalliance treads
And recks not his own rede.
    *Laer.*                    O, fear me not!               55

Enter *Polonius.*

I stay too long. But here my father comes.
A double blessing is a double grace;
Occasion smiles upon a second leave.
    *Pol.* Yet here, Laertes? Aboard, aboard, for shame!
The wind sits in the shoulder of your sail,                    60
And you are stayed for. There—my blessing with thee!
And these few precepts in thy memory
Look thou character. Give thy thoughts no tongue,
Nor any unproportioned thought his act.
Be thou familiar, but by no means vulgar:                      65
Those friends thou hast, and their adoption tried,
Grapple them to thy soul with hoops of steel;
But do not dull thy palm with entertainment
Of each new-hatched, unfledged comrade. Beware
Of entrance to a quarrel; but being in,                        70
Bear't that the opposed may beware of thee.
Give every man thine ear, but few thy voice;
Take each man's censure, but reserve thy judgment.
Costly thy habit as thy purse can buy,

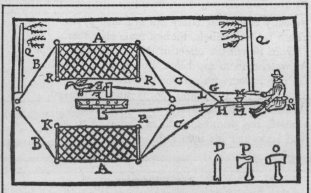

A "springe to catch woodcocks" (snare for fowl).
From Gervase Markham, *Hungers Prevention, or, The Whole Art of Fowling* (1655).

78. **Are most . . . generous:** Nicholas Rowe's emendation. The First Folio reads "Are o a most . . . generous," while the Second Quarto has "Are of a most . . . generall."

81. **husbandry:** thrift, good management

96. **Marry:** a mild oath, derived from "by the Virgin Mary"

100. **'tis put on me:** I am led to believe.

105. **tenders:** offers

But not expressed in fancy; rich, not gaudy;                    75
For the apparel oft proclaims the man,
And they in France of the best rank and station
Are most select and generous, chief in that.
Neither a borrower nor a lender be;
For loan oft loses both itself and friend,                    80
And borrowing dulls the edge of husbandry.
This above all: to thine own self be true,
And it must follow, as the night the day,
Thou canst not then be false to any man.
Farewell. My blessing season this in thee!                    85
   *Laer.* Most humbly do I take my leave, my lord.
   *Pol.* The time invites you. Go, your servants tend.
   *Laer.* Farewell, Ophelia, and remember well
What I have said to you.
   *Oph.*                    'Tis in my memory locked,    90
And you yourself shall keep the key of it.
   *Laer.* Farewell.                                        *Exit.*
   *Pol.* What is't, Ophelia, he hath said to you?
   *Oph.* So please you, something touching the Lord
    Hamlet.                                               95
   *Pol.* Marry, well bethought!
'Tis told me he hath very oft of late
Given private time to you, and you yourself
Have of your audience been most free and bounteous.
If it be so—as so 'tis put on me,                             100
And that in way of caution—I must tell you
You do not understand yourself so clearly
As it behooves my daughter and your honor.
What is between you? Give me up the truth.
   *Oph.* He hath, my lord, of late made many tenders   105
Of his affection to me.

108. **Unsifted:** untried

113-15. **Tender yourself more dearly,/ Or (not to crack the wind of the poor phrase,/ Running it thus) you'll tender me a fool:** offer your company less freely, or (not to force the metaphor until it is winded) you'll offer me a fool for my daughter. **Running** is adopted from a conjecture by John P. Collier; the First Folio has "Roaming" and the Second Quarto "Wrong."

118. **fashion:** fad; see I. iii. 7; **Go to:** come, come; an exclamation of impatience at Ophelia's simplicity

122. **springes:** snares; **woodcocks:** commonly regarded as witless and easily trapped. The name of this animal became synonymous with "dupe," "sucker."

123. **prodigal:** used adverbially; i.e., prodigally

125-26. **extinct in both/ Even in their promise, as it is a-making:** that is, such light and heat as these blazes possess die out almost as soon as they appear.

129-30. **Set your entreatments at a higher rate/ Than a command to parley:** do not grant opportunities for him to woo you at his mere request. The imagery contains military terminology, which since the feudal period was often applied to men's suit for women's love.

132. **larger tether:** more latitude

133. **In few:** in short

134. **brokers:** panders, go-betweens for illicit lovers

135. **Not of that dye which their investments show:** not holy as their clothing would signify. Investments

[continued

136, 137, 138: see next page.

   *Pol.* Affection? Pooh! You speak like a green girl,
Unsifted in such perilous circumstance.
Do you believe his tenders, as you call them?
   *Oph.* I do not know, my lord, what I should think.          110
   *Pol.* Marry, I will teach you! Think yourself a baby
That you have ta'en these tenders for true pay,
Which are not sterling. Tender yourself more dearly,
Or (not to crack the wind of the poor phrase,
Running it thus) you'll tender me a fool.          115
   *Oph.* My lord, he hath importuned me with love
In honorable fashion.
   *Pol.* Ay, fashion you may call it. Go to, go to!
   *Oph.* And hath given countenance to his speech, my
      lord,          120
With almost all the holy vows of heaven.
   *Pol.* Ay, springes to catch woodcocks! I do know,
When the blood burns, how prodigal the soul
Lends the tongue vows. These blazes, daughter,
Giving more light than heat, extinct in both          125
Even in their promise, as it is a-making,
You must not take for fire. From this time
Be somewhat scanter of your maiden presence.
Set your entreatments at a higher rate
Than a command to parley. For Lord Hamlet,          130
Believe so much in him, that he is young,
And with a larger tether may he walk
Than may be given you. In few, Ophelia,
Do not believe his vows; for they are brokers,
Not of that dye which their investments show,          135
But mere implorators of unholy suits,
Breathing like sanctified and pious bawds,
The better to beguile. This is for all:

is used here in a punning fashion, following on **brokers** in the preceding line; "vestments" is the meaning intended.

136. **implorators:** urgers

137. **Breathing like sanctified and pious bawds:** imitating humble piety to mask their true role as bawds (**brokers** as in l. 134). Bawds was suggested by the editor Lewis Theobald; the two original texts read "bonds."

138. **This is for all:** this is my final word.

140. **slander:** misuse disgracefully; **moment leisure:** leisure of a moment

░░░░░░░░░░░░░░░░░░░░░░░░░░░░░░░░░░░

**I. [iv.]** Hamlet, Horatio, and Marcellus keep their vigil. The ghost appears and leads Hamlet out of hearing of his friends, who try to hold him back because they fear the apparition is an evil spirit luring him to damnation.

░░░░░░░░░░░░░░░░░░░░░░░░░

1. **shrewdly:** keenly, intensely

2. **eager:** sharp, from the French *aigre*

8. **held his wont:** was accustomed

10. **doth wake tonight and takes his rouse:** revels all night in a drinking party; see **rouse** at I. ii. 133.

11. **Keeps wassail:** holds a drinking bout; **the swagg'ring upspring reels:** the **upspring** was a German dance, particularly associated with drunken parties. It is unclear whether Hamlet means that the King reels through this dance or merely that the

[continued

12, 14: see next page.

I would not, in plain terms, from this time forth
Have you so slander any moment leisure 140
As to give words or talk with the Lord Hamlet.
Look to't, I charge you. Come your ways.
   *Oph.* I shall obey, my lord.

                          *Exeunt.*

[Scene IV. Elsinore Castle. The platform of the watch.]

Enter *Hamlet, Horatio,* and *Marcellus.*

   *Ham.* The air bites shrewdly; it is very cold.
   *Hor.* It is a nipping and an eager air.
   *Ham.* What hour now?
   *Hor.*           I think it lacks of twelve.
   *Mar.* No, it is struck. 5
   *Hor.* Indeed? I heard it not. It then draws near the
  season
Wherein the spirit held his wont to walk.
         *A flourish of trumpets, and two pieces go off.*
What does this mean, my lord?
   *Ham.* The King doth wake tonight and takes his rouse, 10
Keeps wassail, and the swagg'ring upspring reels,
And, as he drains his draughts of Rhenish down,
The kettledrum and trumpet thus bray out
The triumph of his pledge.
   *Hor.*          Is it a custom? 15
   *Ham.* Ay, marry, is't;
But to my mind, though I am native here

dance "reels" as an accompaniment to the drinking.

12. **Rhenish**: Rhine wine

14. **triumph of his pledge**: it was customary to pledge a health and then drain the drinking cup at one swallow. Hamlet is sarcastic in calling the ability to do so a triumph.

19. **breach**: neglect

21. **traduced and taxed**: defamed and censured

22. **clepe**: call

23. **addition**: title

25. **The pith and marrow**: synonymous words; the very essence; **attribute**: reputation

27. **mole of nature**: natural fault

30. **o'ergrowth of some complexion**: extravagant development of some trait, such as melancholy

31. **pales and forts**: synonymous; limits or bounds

32. **o'erleavens**: transforms

33. **plausive**: pleasing

35. **nature's livery**: the uniform bestowed by nature; **fortune's star**: an endowment determined by fate

36. **Their virtues else**: their other virtues

38. **censure**: opinion only, not criticism; see I. iii. 73.

39. **dram**: small amount; **e'il**: evil

40. **dout**: literally, put out; that is, efface. Often dout is George Steevens' suggestion for the phrase "of a doubt" in the early texts.

41. **To his own scandal**: to the extent that he is completely disgraced

And to the manner born, it is a custom
More honored in the breach than the observance.
This heavy-headed revel east and west                20
Makes us traduced and taxed of other nations;
They clepe us drunkards and with swinish phrase
Soil our addition; and indeed it takes
From our achievements, though performed at height,
The pith and marrow of our attribute.                25
So oft it chances in particular men
That for some vicious mole of nature in them,
As in their birth,—wherein they are not guilty,
Since nature cannot choose his origin,—
By their o'ergrowth of some complexion,                30
Oft breaking down the pales and forts of reason,
Or by some habit that too much o'erleavens
The form of plausive manners, that these men
Carrying, I say, the stamp of one defect,
Being nature's livery, or fortune's star,                35
Their virtues else—be they as pure as grace,
As infinite as man may undergo—
Shall in the general censure take corruption
From that particular fault. The dram of e'il
Doth all the noble substance often dout                40
To his own scandal.

### Enter *Ghost*.

  *Hor.*              Look, my lord, it comes!
  *Ham.* Angels and ministers of grace defend us!
Be thou a spirit of health or goblin damned,
Bring with thee airs from heaven or blasts from hell,                45
Be thy intents wicked or charitable,

51. **canonized:** sanctified by burial in accordance with prescribed holy rites

52. **Cerements:** graveclothes

58. **we fools of nature:** we humans, who become as fools before supernatural phenomena

59-60. **So horridly to shake . . . souls:** the dead **corse** (l. 56) causes them to wonder fearfully at a phenomenon so beyond human understanding.

63. **impartment:** disclosure

Thou com'st in such a questionable shape
That I will speak to thee. I'll call thee Hamlet,
King, father, royal Dane. O, answer me!
Let me not burst in ignorance, but tell                               50
Why thy canonized bones, hearsed in death,
Have burst their cerements; why the sepulchre
Wherein we saw thee quietly inurned,
Hath oped his ponderous and marble jaws
To cast thee up again. What may this mean                             55
That thou, dead corse, again in complete steel,
Revisits thus the glimpses of the moon,
Making night hideous, and we fools of nature
So horridly to shake our disposition
With thoughts beyond the reaches of our souls?                        60
Say, why is this? wherefore? What should we do?
                              *Ghost beckons Hamlet.*
  *Hor.* It beckons you to go away with it,
As if it some impartment did desire
To you alone.
  *Mar.*          Look with what courteous action                     65
It waves you to a more removed ground.
But do not go with it!
  *Hor.*                No, by no means!
  *Ham.* It will not speak. Then will I follow it.
  *Hor.* Do not, my lord!                                             70
  *Ham.*                Why, what should be the fear?
I do not set my life at a pin's fee;
And for my soul, what can it do to that,
Being a thing immortal as itself?
It waves me forth again. I'll follow it.                              75
  *Hor.* What if it tempt you toward the flood, my lord,
Or to the dreadful summit of the cliff

80. **deprive your sovereignty of reason:** take away the supremacy of your reason

82. **toys of desperation:** desperate fancies

93. **the Nemean lion:** a beast credited with invulnerability, slain by Hercules as one of his twelve labors

95. **lets:** hinders

That beetles o'er his base into the sea,
And there assume some other, horrible form
Which might deprive your sovereignty of reason          80
And draw you into madness? Think of it.
The very place puts toys of desperation,
Without more motive, into every brain
That looks so many fathoms to the sea
And hears it roar beneath.          85

*Ham.*          It waves me still.
Co on, I'll follow thee.

*Mar.* You shall not go, my lord.

*Ham.*          Hold off your hands!

*Hor.* Be ruled, you shall not go.          90

*Ham.*          My fate cries out
And makes each petty artery in this body
As hardy as the Nemean lion's nerve.

                    [*Ghost beckons.*]
Still am I called. Unhand me, gentlemen—
By heaven, I'll make a ghost of him that lets me!          95
I say, away!—Go on, I'll follow thee.

                    *Exeunt Ghost and Hamlet.*

*Hor.* He waxes desperate with imagination.

*Mar.* Let's follow; 'tis not fit thus to obey him.

*Hor.* Have after. To what issue will this come?

*Mar.* Something is rotten in the state of Denmark.          100

*Hor.* Heaven will direct it.

*Mar.*          Nay, let's follow him.

                    *Exeunt.*

The "fretful porpentine."
From Henry Topsell, *History of Four-Footed Beasts* (1658).

**I. [v.]** The ghost has led Hamlet to another part
of the battlements, where he reveals himself as the
spirit of Hamlet's father and commands him to
avenge his murder. To Hamlet's horrified ears, the
ghost unfolds the story of how Claudius, who had
already seduced his wife, poisoned him while he
slept. He urges Hamlet to punish his murderer but
to spare Gertrude.

Hamlet refuses to tell his friends what passed between him and the ghost and forces them to swear
on his sword that they will reveal nothing of what
they have seen, regardless of how he may act in
the future. The ghost, out of sight, adds his own
urging, and they swear.

25. **porpentine:** porcupine

26

[Scene V. Same. Another part of the ramparts.]

Enter *Ghost* and *Hamlet*.

*Ham.* Whither wilt thou lead me? Speak, I'll go no
    further.
*Ghost.* Mark me.
*Ham.*           I will.
*Ghost.*               My hour is almost come,      5
When I to sulph'rous and tormenting flames
Must render up myself.
*Ham.*             Alas, poor ghost!
*Ghost.* Pity me not, but lend thy serious hearing
To what I shall unfold.                          10
*Ham.*            Speak, I am bound to hear.
*Ghost.* So art thou to revenge, when thou shalt hear.
*Ham.* What?
*Ghost.* I am thy father's spirit,
Doomed for a certain term to walk the night,      15
And for the day confined to fast in fires,
Till the foul crimes done in my days of nature
Are burnt and purged away. But that I am forbid
To tell the secrets of my prison house,
I could a tale unfold whose lightest word        20
Would harrow up thy soul, freeze thy young blood,
Make thy two eyes, like stars, start from their spheres,
Thy knotted and combined locks to part,
And each particular hair to stand on end
Like quills upon the fretful porpentine.         25

26. **eternal blazon:** disclosure of the conditions of eternity

38. **fat:** thick and sluggish

39. **Lethe wharf:** the shores of the Lethe, a river in Hades, the waters of which provided complete forgetfulness to departed souls

43. **process:** relation

44. **Rankly abused:** utterly deceived

49. **adulterate:** adulterous

But this eternal blazon must not be
To ears of flesh and blood. List, list, O, list!
If thou didst ever thy dear father love—
    *Ham.* O God!
    *Ghost.* Revenge his foul and most unnatural murder.   30
    *Ham.* Murder?
    *Ghost.* Murder most foul, as in the best it is;
But this most foul, strange, and unnatural.
    *Ham.* Haste me to know't, that I, with wings as swift
As meditation or the thoughts of love,   35
May sweep to my revenge.
    *Ghost.*              I find thee apt;
And duller shouldst thou be than the fat weed
That rots itself in ease on Lethe wharf,
Wouldst thou not stir in this. Now, Hamlet, hear:   40
'Tis given out that, sleeping in my orchard,
A serpent stung me; so the whole ear of Denmark
Is by a forged process of my death
Rankly abused; but know, thou noble youth,
The serpent that did sting thy father's life   45
Now wears his crown.
    *Ham.*          O my prophetic soul!
My uncle?
    *Ghost.* Ay, that incestuous, that adulterate beast,
With witchcraft of his wit, with traitorous gifts—   50
O wicked wit and gifts, that have the power
So to seduce!—won to his shameful lust
The will of my most seeming-virtuous queen.
O Hamlet, what a falling-off was there,
From me, whose love was of that dignity   55
That it went hand in hand even with the vow
I made to her in marriage, and to decline

68. **Upon my secure hour:** when I was unsuspecting. **Secure** means here not literally "safe" but unmindful of danger.

69. **hebenon:** no such plant or poison is known. Christopher Marlowe refers to "juice of hebon" in *The Jew of Malta* and Shakespeare may have remembered it as a picturesque word for a poisonous plant.

71. **leperous:** so-called because of its effect, described in l. 79

75. **posset:** curdle

76. **eager:** sharp; see I. [iv.] 2.

78. **tetter:** skin eruption; **barked about:** covered, like a bark

79. **lazar-like:** like a leper

82. **dispatched:** rid of; that is, deprived of

84. **Unhous'led:** without benefit of the last sacrament; **disappointed:** not prepared, by confession, for eternity; **unaneled:** not anointed in the sacrament of extreme unction

Upon a wretch whose natural gifts were poor
To those of mine!
But virtue, as it never will be moved,                               60
Though lewdness court it in a shape of heaven,
So lust, though to a radiant angel linked,
Will sate itself in a celestial bed
And prey on garbage.
But soft! methinks I scent the morning air.                          65
Brief let me be. Sleeping within my orchard,
My custom always of the afternoon,
Upon my secure hour thy uncle stole,
With juice of cursed hebenon in a vial,
And in the porches of my ears did pour                               70
The leperous distilment, whose effect
Holds such an enmity with blood of man
That swift as quicksilver it courses through
The natural gates and alleys of the body,
And with a sudden vigor it doth posset                               75
And curd, like eager droppings into milk,
The thin and wholesome blood; so did it mine,
And a most instant tetter barked about,
Most lazar-like, with vile and loathsome crust
All my smooth body.                                                  80
Thus was I, sleeping, by a brother's hand
Of life, of crown, of queen, at once dispatched;
Cut off even in the blossoms of my sin,
Unhous'led, disappointed, unaneled,
No reck'ning made, but sent to my account                            85
With all my imperfections on my head.
   *Ham.* O, horrible! O, horrible! most horrible!
   *Ghost.* If thou hast nature in thee, bear it not.
Let not the royal bed of Denmark be

90. **luxury:** lustful indulgence

96. **matin:** morning

104. **this distracted globe:** Hamlet presses his hand to his head.

105. **table:** tablet; see **tables** at l. 114.

106. **fond:** foolish

107. **saws:** maxims; **forms:** images; **pressures:** impressions

108. **youth and observation:** youthful observation

117. **word:** motto, the word which will guide my future action

A couch for luxury and damned incest.                              90
But, howsoever thou pursuest this act,
Taint not thy mind, nor let thy soul contrive
Against thy mother aught. Leave her to heaven,
And to those thorns that in her bosom lodge
To prick and sting her. Fare thee well at once,        95
The glowworm shows the matin to be near
And gins to pale his uneffectual fire.
Adieu, adieu, adieu! Remember me.                *Exit.*
   *Ham.* O all you host of heaven! O earth! What else?
And shall I couple hell? O fie! Hold, hold, my heart!   100
And you, my sinews, grow not instant old,
But bear me stiffly up. Remember thee?
Ay, thou poor ghost, while memory holds a seat
In this distracted globe. Remember thee?
Yea, from the table of my memory                        105
I'll wipe away all trivial fond records,
All saws of books, all forms, all pressures past
That youth and observation copied there,
And thy commandment all alone shall live
Within the book and volume of my brain,                 110
Unmixed with baser matter. Yes, by heaven!
O most pernicious woman!
O villain, villain, smiling, damned villain!
My tables, my tables! Meet it is I set it down
That one may smile, and smile, and be a villain;        115
At least I'm sure it may be so in Denmark.    [*Writes.*]
So, uncle, there you are. Now to my word:
It is "Adieu, adieu! Remember me."
I have sworn't.
   *Hor.* (*Within*) My lord, my lord!                   120

125. **Hillo, ho, ho, boy**: Hamlet mocks Marcellus' hail with the conventional call used by the falconer to his bird.

138. **arrant**: unqualified

143. **circumstance**: ceremony, ado

Enter *Horatio* and *Marcellus*.

*Mar.*                          Lord Hamlet!
*Hor.*                               Heaven secure him!
*Ham.* So be it!
*Mar.* Illo, ho, ho, my lord!
*Ham.* Hillo, ho, ho, boy! Come, bird, come.           125
*Mar.* How is't, my noble lord?
*Hor.*                     What news, my lord?
*Ham.* O, wonderful!
*Hor.* Good my lord, tell it.
*Ham.*                     No, you'll reveal it.         130
*Hor.* Not I, my lord, by heaven!
*Mar.*                     Nor I, my lord.
*Ham.* How say you then? Would heart of man once
   think it?
But you'll be secret?                                    135
*Both.*          Ay, by heaven, my lord.
*Ham.* There's ne'er a villain dwelling in all Denmark
But he's an arrant knave.
*Hor.* There needs no ghost, my lord, come from the
   grave                                                 140
To tell us this.
*Ham.*      Why, right! You are in the right!
And so, without more circumstance at all,
I hold it fit that we shake hands and part;
You, as your business and desires shall point you,      145
For every man hath business and desire,
Such as it is; and for my own poor part,
Look you, I'll go pray.
*Hor.* These are but wild and whirling words, my lord.

155. **an honest ghost:** that is, no demon in disguise

167. **Upon my sword:** an oath on a sword would have special force, since the hilt and blade formed a cross.

172-73. **truepenny:** an Elizabethan expression meaning approximately "good fellow"

*Ham.* I am sorry they offend you, heartily;                    150
Yes, faith, heartily.

*Hor.*              There's no offense, my lord.

*Ham.* Yes, by Saint Patrick, but there is, Horatio,
And much offense too. Touching this vision here,
It is an honest ghost, that let me tell you.                    155
For your desire to know what is between us,
O'ermaster't as you may. And now, good friends,
As you are friends, scholars, and soldiers,
Give me one poor request.

*Hor.* What is't, my lord? We will.                    160

*Ham.* Never make known what you have seen tonight.

*Both.* My lord, we will not.

*Ham.*                    Nay, but swear't.

*Hor.*                              In faith,
My lord, not I.                    165

*Mar.*          Nor I, my lord—in faith.

*Ham.* Upon my sword.

*Mar.*                    We have sworn, my lord, al-
    ready.

*Ham.* Indeed, upon my sword, indeed.                    170

*Ghost cries under the stage.*

*Ghost.* Swear.

*Ham.* Aha boy, say'st thou so? Art thou there, true-
    penny?
Come on! You hear this fellow in the cellarage.
Consent to swear.                    175

*Hor.*          Propose the oath, my lord.

*Ham.* Never to speak of this that you have seen.
Swear by my sword.

180. **Hic et ubique:** here and everywhere

188. **pioner:** pioneer, miner

190. **as a stranger give it welcome:** give it the courteous welcome due a stranger.

192. **your philosophy:** natural philosophy or science, not Horatio's personal philosophy

199. **With arms encumb'red thus, or this headshake:** folding the arms or shaking the head in a knowing way

203. **list to speak:** cared to speak

204. **giving out:** hint

*Ghost.* [*Beneath*] Swear.
  *Ham.* Hic et ubique? Then we'll shift our ground.    180
Come hither, gentlemen,
And lay your hands again upon my sword.
Never to speak of this that you have heard:
Swear by my sword.
  *Ghost.* [*Beneath*] Swear by his sword.            185
  *Ham.* Well said, old mole! Canst work i' the earth so
    fast?
A worthy pioner! Once more remove, good friends.
  *Hor.* O day and night, but this is wondrous strange!
  *Ham.* And therefore as a stranger give it welcome.    190
There are more things in heaven and earth, Horatio,
Than are dreamt of in your philosophy.
But come!
Here, as before, never, so help you mercy,
How strange or odd soe'er I bear myself                          195
(As I perchance hereafter shall think meet
To put an antic disposition on),
That you, at such times seeing me, never shall,
With arms encumb'red thus, or this head-shake,
Or by pronouncing of some doubtful phrase,                       200
As "Well, well, we know," or "We could, an if we
    would,"
Or "If we list to speak," or "There be, an if they might,"
Or such ambiguous giving out, to note
That you know aught of me—this not to do,                        205
So grace and mercy at your most need help you,
Swear.
  *Ghost.* [*Beneath*] Swear.
                            [*They swear.*]

214. **still**: always; see I. ii. 110.

*Ham.* Rest, rest, perturbed spirit! So, gentlemen,
With all my love I do commend me to you;                210
And what so poor a man as Hamlet is
May do t' express his love and friending to you,
God willing, shall not lack. Let us go in together;
And still your fingers on your lips, I pray.
The time is out of joint. O cursed spite              215
That ever I was born to set it right!
Nay, come, let's go together.

                                        *Exeunt.*

THE TRAGEDY OF

# HAMLET,

PRINCE OF DENMARK

ACT II

**II. [i.]** Polonius directs an attendant to take Laertes fresh funds and to spy on his activities in France to determine whether he is leading too wild a life.

Ophelia enters and reports that Hamlet, showing all the symptoms of madness, has just visited her in her chamber. Polonius immediately decides that Hamlet is mad for love of Ophelia and hurries her off to report the matter to the King.

||||||||||||||||||||||||||||||||||||

3. **marvell's:** marvellous
8. **Danskers:** Danes
11. **encompassment and drift of question:** roundabout inquiry
13. **particular demands:** direct questions
20. **put on him:** charge him with

# ACT II

[Scene I. Elsinore. *Polonius'* house.]

Enter *Polonius* and *Reynaldo*.

*Pol.* Give him this money and these notes, Reynaldo.

*Rey.* I will, my lord.

*Pol.* You shall do marvell's wisely, good Reynaldo,
Before you visit him, to make inquire
Of his behavior.                                                5

*Rey.*         My lord, I did intend it.

*Pol.* Marry, well said, very well said. Look you, sir,
Enquire me first what Danskers are in Paris;
And how, and who, what means, and where they keep,
What company, at what expense; and finding              10
By this encompassment and drift of question
That they do know my son, come you more nearer
Than your particular demands will touch it.
Take you, as 'twere, some distant knowledge of him;
As thus, "I know his father and his friends,                15
And in part him." Do you mark this, Reynaldo?

*Rey.* Ay, very well, my lord.

*Pol.* "And in part him, but," you may say, "not well.
But if't be he I mean, he's very wild,
Addicted so and so"; and there put on him               20

34

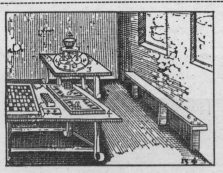

Games of chance.
From Comenius, *Orbis sensualium picti* (1685).

21. **forgeries:** fabrications; **rank:** great

23. **wanton:** unrestrained

28. **Drabbing:** consorting with loose women

30. **season it in the charge:** soften the seriousness of the charge by your manner of describing it

32. **open to incontinency:** given to excessive indulgence in any pleasure

33. **quaintly:** skillfully, cleverly

34. **taints of liberty:** faults resulting from freedom

36. **unreclaimed:** untamed

37. **Of general assault:** common to youth generally

43. **fetch of warrant:** guaranteed device

45. **a little soiled i' the working:** that is, as cloth may be soiled with handling in making a garment

48. **prenominate:** previously named

50. **closes with you in this consequence:** agrees with you as follows

35

What forgeries you please; marry, none so rank
As may dishonor him—take heed of that;
But, sir, such wanton, wild, and usual slips
As are companions noted and most known
To youth and liberty.                                      25
    *Rey.*          As gaming, my lord.
    *Pol.* Ay, or drinking, fencing, swearing, quarrelling,
Drabbing. You may go so far.
    *Rey.* My lord, that would dishonor him.
    *Pol.* Faith, no, as you may season it in the charge.     30
You must not put another scandal on him,
That he is open to incontinency.
That's not my meaning. But breathe his faults so quaintly
That they may seem the taints of liberty,
The flash and outbreak of a fiery mind,                    35
A savageness in unreclaimed blood,
Of general assault.
    *Rey.*        But, my good lord—
    *Pol.* Wherefore should you do this?
    *Rey.*                Ay, my lord,     40
I would know that.
    *Pol.*       Marry, sir, here's my drift,
And I believe it is a fetch of warrant.
You laying these slight sullies on my son
As 'twere a thing a little soiled i' the working,          45
Mark you,
Your party in converse, him you would sound,
Having ever seen in the prenominate crimes
The youth you breathe of guilty, be assured
He closes with you in this consequence:                    50
"Good sir," or so, or "friend," or "gentleman"—

A tennis match.
From Comenius, *Orbis sensualium picti* (1685).

52. **addition**: title; see I. [iv.] 23.

64. **o'ertook in 's rouse**: overcome by drink

67. **Videlicet**: that is to say

70. **reach**: comprehension

71. **windlasses and . . . assays of bias**: winding turns and oblique approaches. The latter is a term from bowling.

78. **in yourself**: with your own eyes

80. **ply his music**: indulge his fancy as he will. In other words, Reynaldo is not to correct Laertes' behavior; he is only to note it and report to Polonius.

According to the phrase or the addition
Of man and country—
    *Rey.*             Very good, my lord.
    *Pol.* And then, sir, does he this—he does—What was I   55
about to say? By the mass, I was about to say something!
Where did I leave?
    *Rey.* At "closes in the consequence," at "friend or so,"
and "gentleman."
    *Pol.* At "closes in the consequence"—Ay, marry!     60
He closes thus: "I know the gentleman.
I saw him yesterday, or t'other day,
Or then, or then, with such or such; and, as you say,
There was he gaming; there o'ertook in 's rouse;
There falling out at tennis"; or perchance,     65
"I saw him enter such a house of sale,"
Videlicet, a brothel, or so forth.
See you now—
Your bait of falsehood takes this carp of truth;
And thus do we of wisdom and of reach,     70
With windlasses and with assays of bias,
By indirections find directions out.
So, by my former lecture and advice,
Shall you my son. You have me, have you not?
    *Rey.* My lord, I have.     75
    *Pol.*               God be wi' you, fare you well!
    *Rey.* Good my lord!
    *Pol.* Observe his inclination in yourself.
    *Rey.* I shall, my lord.
    *Pol.* And let him ply his music.     80
    *Rey.*               Well, my lord.
    *Pol.* Farewell!

                                    *Exit Reynaldo.*

86. **closet:** boudoir

87. **doublet:** a jacket, which formed the main garment of male dress; **all unbraced:** completely open

89. **down-gyved:** fallen in coils

Enter *Ophelia*.

    How now, Ophelia? What's the matter?
*Oph.* O my lord, my lord, I have been so affrighted!
*Pol.* With what, i' the name of God?                    85
*Oph.* My lord, as I was sewing in my closet,
Lord Hamlet, with his doublet all unbraced,
No hat upon his head, his stockings fouled,
Ungart'red, and down-gyved to his ankle;
Pale as his shirt, his knees knocking each other,      90
And with a look so piteous in purport
As if he had been loosed out of hell
To speak of horrors—he comes before me.
    *Pol.* Mad for thy love?
    *Oph.*                My lord, I do not know,       95
But truly I do fear it.
    *Pol.*            What said he?
    *Oph.* He took me by the wrist and held me hard;
Then goes he to the length of all his arm,
And, with his other hand thus o'er his brow,          100
He falls to such perusal of my face
As he would draw it. Long stayed he so.
At last, a little shaking of mine arm,
And thrice his head thus waving up and down,
He raised a sigh so piteous and profound              105
As it did seem to shatter all his bulk
And end his being. That done, he lets me go,
And with his head over his shoulder turned
He seemed to find his way without his eyes,
For out o' doors he went without their help           110
And to the last bended their light on me.

113. **ecstasy:** madness
114. **property:** characteristic; **fordoes:** destroys
124. **quoted:** noted
125. **beshrew:** curse; **jealousy:** suspicion
126. **our age:** that is, old men like me
127. **cast beyond ourselves:** be overly cautious

130-32. **which, being kept close, might move/
More grief to hide than hate to utter love:** might cause more grief by its concealment than distaste in the King and Queen at hearing of Hamlet's love for someone of lower rank

*Pol.* Come, go with me. I will go seek the King.
This is the very ecstasy of love,
Whose violent property fordoes itself
And leads the will to desperate undertakings          115
As oft as any passion under heaven
That does afflict our natures. I am sorry.
What, have you given him any hard words of late?
   *Oph.* No, my good lord; but, as you did command,
I did repel his letters and denied          120
His access to me.
   *Pol.*          That hath made him mad.
I am sorry that with better heed and judgment
I had not quoted him. I feared he did but trifle
And meant to wrack thee; but beshrew my jealousy!          125
By heaven, it is as proper to our age
To cast beyond ourselves in our opinions
As it is common for the younger sort
To lack discretion. Come, go we to the King.
This must be known; which, being kept close, might          130
    move
More grief to hide than hate to utter love.
Come.
                        *Exeunt.*

**II. ii.** Claudius and Gertrude welcome two old friends of Hamlet, Rosencrantz and Guildenstern, summoned to observe Hamlet and determine the cause of his "antic disposition."

The ambassadors from Norway report a successful mission. Polonius presents his theory that disappointed love for Ophelia has unhinged Hamlet's mind. Claudius is unconvinced but agrees to Polonius' plan to observe unseen a meeting between Ophelia and Hamlet.

Hamlet welcomes Rosencrantz and Guildenstern and immediately suspects that they are Claudius' spies.

A company of players arrive. Hamlet arranges a performance of *The Murder of Gonzago* with some lines of his own inserted. Alone, he expresses self-contempt because he has done nothing to avenge his father. Time has weakened the effect of the ghost's revelation and he now feels the need to reassure himself that it was a true ghost and not a devil. He decides to use the play to test the King's conscience.

6. **Sith:** since
13. **vouchsafe your rest:** deign to stay
18. **opened:** revealed
22. **gentry:** courtesy

Scene II. [Elsinore. A room in the Castle.]

*Flourish.* Enter *King* and *Queen, Rosencrantz,* and
    *Guildenstern,* cum aliis.

*King.* Welcome, dear Rosencrantz and Guildenstern.
Moreover that we much did long to see you,
The need we have to use you did provoke
Our hasty sending. Something have you heard
Of Hamlet's transformation. So I call it,                    5
Sith nor the exterior nor the inward man
Resembles that it was. What it should be,
More than his father's death, that thus hath put him
So much from the understanding of himself,
I cannot dream of. I entreat you both                        10
That, being of so young days brought up with him,
And since so neighbored to his youth and havior,
That you vouchsafe your rest here in our court
Some little time; so by your companies
To draw him on to pleasures, and to gather                   15
So much as from occasion you may glean,
Whether aught to us unknown afflicts him thus
That, opened, lies within our remedy.
    *Queen.* Good gentlemen, he hath much talked of you,
And sure I am two men there are not living                   20
To whom he more adheres. If it will please you
To show us so much gentry and good will
As to expend your time with us awhile
For the supply and profit of our hope,
Your visitation shall receive such thanks                    25
As fits a king's remembrance.

32. **in the full bent:** to the utmost; from archery, picturing a bow bent to its limit

50. **Hunts not the trail of policy so sure:** is not as sure in cunning

*Ros.*                    Both your Majesties
Might, by the sovereign power you have of us,
Put your dread pleasures more into command
Than to entreaty.                                        30
    *Guil.*        But we both obey,
And here give up ourselves, in the full bent,
To lay our service freely at your feet,
To be commanded.
    *King.* Thanks, Rosencrantz and gentle Guildenstern.   35
    *Queen.* Thanks, Guildenstern and gentle Rosencrantz.
And I beseech you instantly to visit
My too much changed son.—Go, some of you,
And bring these gentlemen where Hamlet is.
    *Guil.* Heavens make our presence and our practices   40
Pleasant and helpful to him!
    *Queen.*                    Ay, amen!
        *Exeunt Rosencrantz and Guildenstern, [with some
                                Attendants].*
                *Enter Polonius.*

*Pol.* The ambassadors from Norway, my good lord,
Are joyfully returned.
    *King.* Thou still hast been the father of good news.   45
    *Pol.* Have I, my lord? Assure you, my good liege,
I hold my duty as I hold my soul,
Both to my God and to my gracious king;
And I do think—or else this brain of mine
Hunts not the trail of policy so sure                       50
As it hath used to do—that I have found
The very cause of Hamlet's lunacy.
    *King.* O, speak of that! That do I long to hear.

55. **fruit:** dessert

56. **grace:** honor; see use at I. ii. 130.

59. **the main:** the main subject that has preoccupied him

61. **sift:** question closely

71. **borne in hand:** deceived

*Pol.* Give first admittance to the ambassadors,
My news shall be the fruit to that great feast.                    55
    *King.* Thyself do grace to them, and bring them in.
                                        [*Exit Polonius.*]
He tells me, my dear Gertrude, he hath found
The head and source of all your son's distemper.
    *Queen.* I doubt it is no other but the main,
His father's death and our o'erhasty marriage.                     60
    *King.* Well, we shall sift him.

        Enter *Polonius, Voltemand,* and *Cornelius.*

                        Welcome, my good friends.
Say, Voltemand, what from our brother Norway?
    *Volt.* Most fair return of greetings and desires.
Upon our first, he sent out to suppress                            65
His nephew's levies, which to him appeared
To be a preparation 'gainst the Polack,
But better looked into, he truly found
It was against your Highness; whereat grieved,
That so his sickness, age, and impotence                           70
Was falsely borne in hand, sends out arrests
On Fortinbras; which he, in brief, obeys,
Receives rebuke from Norway, and, in fine,
Makes vow before his uncle never more
To give the assay of arms against your Majesty.                    75
Whereon old Norway, overcome with joy,
Gives him three thousand crowns in annual fee
And his commission to employ those soldiers,
So levied as before, against the Polack;
With an entreaty, herein further shown,                            80
                                        [*Gives a paper.*]

83. **On such regards of safety and allowance:** according to such terms as you think safe and permissible

85. **likes:** pleases

86. **at our more considered time:** when we have time for suitable consideration

92. **expostulate:** discourse upon

96. **wit:** understanding, wisdom

105. **figure:** rhetorical device

That it might please you to give quiet pass
Through your dominions for this enterprise,
On such regards of safety and allowance
As therein are set down.

   *King.*               It likes us well;        85
And at our more considered time we'll read,
Answer, and think upon this business.
Meantime we thank you for your well-took labor.
Go to your rest; at night we'll feast together.
Most welcome home!       *Exeunt Ambassadors.*  90

   *Pol.*          This business is well ended.
My liege, and madam, to expostulate
What majesty should be, what duty is,
Why day is day, night night, and time is time,
Were nothing but to waste night, day, and time.     95
Therefore, since brevity is the soul of wit,
And tediousness the limbs and outward flourishes,
I will be brief. Your noble son is mad.
Mad call I it; for, to define true madness,
What is't but to be nothing else but mad?     100
But let that go.

   *Queen.*    More matter, with less art.

   *Pol.* Madam, I swear I use no art at all.
That he is mad, 'tis true: 'tis true 'tis pity;
And pity 'tis 'tis true. A foolish figure!     105
But farewell it, for I will use no art.
Mad let us grant him then. And now remains
That we find out the cause of this effect—
Or rather say, the cause of this defect,
For this effect defective comes by cause.     110
Thus it remains, and the remainder thus.

112. **Perpend:** consider

116. **beautified:** beautiful. Hamlet meant the word as a sincere tribute, though to Polonius it suggests artificial beauty.

128. **ill at these numbers:** untalented at rhyming thus

129. **reckon my groans:** sum up my lover's woe

131-32. **whilst this machine is to him:** while I still possess this body

134-36. **hath his solicitings . . . All given to mine ear:** that is, she has reported all his attentions to her.

Perpend:
I have a daughter (have while she is mine),
Who in her duty and obedience, mark,
Hath given me this. Now gather, and surmise.                   115
                                    [*Reads*] *the letter.*

*To the celestial, and my soul's idol, the most beautified*
   *Ophelia,—*

That's an ill phrase, a vile phrase; "beautified" is a vile
   phrase.
But you shall hear. Thus:                          [*Reads*]  120

*In her excellent white bosom, these, &c.*

   *Queen.* Came this from Hamlet to her?
   *Pol.* Good madam, stay awhile. I will be faithful.
                                            [*Reads*]

      *Doubt thou the stars are fire;*
         *Doubt that the sun doth move;*               125
      *Doubt truth to be a liar;*
         *But never doubt I love.*

*O dear Ophelia, I am ill at these numbers; I have not*
*art to reckon my groans; but that I love thee best, O most*
*best, believe it. Adieu.*                              130
      *Thine evermore, most dear lady, whilst this machine*
                        *is to him,* HAMLET.

This, in obedience, hath my daughter shown me;
And more above, hath his solicitings,
As they fell out by time, by means, and place,          135
All given to mine ear.

141. **would fain:** would willingly

146. **played the desk or table book:** acted passively as a storage receptacle for the information

147. **given my heart a winking:** felt no concern

148. **idle:** fruitless, without being moved to action

149. **round:** bluntly, without beating around the bush

155. **took the fruits of my advice:** did as I told her

158. **watch:** sleepless state

159. **declension:** deterioration

*King.*　　　　But how hath she
Received his love?
　*Pol.*　　　What do you think of me?
　*King.* As of a man faithful and honorable.　　　　140
　*Pol.* I would fain prove so. But what might you think,
When I had seen this hot love on the wing
(As I perceived it, I must tell you that,
Before my daughter told me), what might you,
Or my dear Majesty your queen here, think,　　　　145
If I had played the desk or table book,
Or given my heart a winking, mute and dumb,
Or looked upon this love with idle sight?
What might you think? No, I went round to work
And my young mistress thus I did bespeak:　　　　150
"Lord Hamlet is a prince, out of thy star.
This must not be." And then I precepts gave her,
That she should lock herself from his resort,
Admit no messengers, receive no tokens.
Which done, she took the fruits of my advice,　　　　155
And he, repulsed, a short tale to make,
Fell into a sadness, then into a fast,
Thence to a watch, thence into a weakness,
Thence to a lightness, and, by this declension,
Into the madness wherein now he raves,　　　　160
And all we mourn for.
　*King.*　　　　Do you think 'tis this?
　*Queen.* It may be, very like.
　*Pol.* Hath there been such a time—I would fain know
　　that—　　　　165
That I have positively said " 'Tis so,"
When it proved otherwise?

173. **the centre:** the heart of the earth

175. **four:** an indefinite number, a common usage of the time

179. **arras:** wall hanging

188. **board:** accost

192. **You are a fishmonger:** Hamlet intends Polonius to think this sheer madness, but he may be thinking of Erysichthon's daughter, in Ovid's story. To prevent her recognition by the man to whom Erysichthon sold her, Neptune, who had loved the girl, changed her to a fisherman (Ovid, *Metamorphoses*, Book VIII). Elsewhere Polonius reminds Hamlet of Jephthah, another man who sacrificed his daughter.

*King.*                    Not that I know.

*Pol.* [*Points to his head and shoulder.*] Take this from
    this, if this be otherwise.                    170
If circumstances lead me, I will find
Where truth is hid, though it were hid indeed
Within the centre.

*King.*              How may we try it further?

*Pol.* You know sometimes he walks four hours together 175
Here in the lobby.

*Queen.*           So he does indeed.

*Pol.* At such a time I'll loose my daughter to him.
Be you and I behind an arras then.
Mark the encounter. If he love her not,                    180
And be not from his reason fall'n thereon,
Let me be no assistant for a state,
But keep a farm and carters.

*King.*                    We will try it.


Enter *Hamlet*, reading on a book.


*Queen.* But look where sadly the poor wretch comes 185
    reading.

*Pol.* Away, I do beseech you, both away!
I'll board him presently. O, give me leave.
            *Exeunt King and Queen,* [*with Attendants*].
How does my good Lord Hamlet?

*Ham.* Well, God-a-mercy.                    190

*Pol.* Do you know me, my lord?

*Ham.* Excellent well. You are a fishmonger.

*Pol.* Not I, my lord.

*Ham.* Then I would you were so honest a man.

200. **a god:** William Warburton's emendation for "good" in the early texts; a reference to the sun god of classical mythology. Elizabethan belief held that maggots and other organisms were generated directly by the sun.

202. **Let her not walk i' the sun:** that is, lest she conceive to her dishonor

205. **by:** about

219. **honesty:** honorable conduct

*Pol.* Honest, my lord? 195

*Ham.* Ay, sir. To be honest, as this world goes, is to be one man picked out of ten thousand.

*Pol.* That's very true, my lord.

*Ham.* For if the sun breed maggots in a dead dog, being a god kissing carrion—Have you a daughter? 200

*Pol.* I have, my lord.

*Ham.* Let her not walk i' the sun. Conception is a blessing, but not as your daughter may conceive. Friend, look to't.

*Pol.* [*Aside*] How say you by that? Still harping on 205 my daughter. Yet he knew me not at first. He said I was a fishmonger. He is far gone, far gone! And truly in my youth I suff'red much extremity for love—very near this. I'll speak to him again.—What do you read, my lord?

*Ham.* Words, words, words. 210

*Pol.* What is the matter, my lord?

*Ham.* Between who?

*Pol.* I mean, the matter that you read, my lord.

*Ham.* Slanders, sir; for the satirical rogue says here that old men have grey beards; that their faces are wrin- 215 kled; their eyes purging thick amber and plum-tree gum; and that they have a plentiful lack of wit, together with most weak hams. All which, sir, though I most power- fully and potently believe, yet I hold it not honesty to have it thus set down; for you yourself, sir, should be old 220 as I am if, like a crab, you could go backward.

*Pol.* [*Aside*] Though this be madness, yet there is method in't.—Will you walk out of the air, my lord?

*Ham.* Into my grave?

*Pol.* Indeed, that is out o' the air. [*Aside*] How preg- 225

226. **happiness:** aptness
244. **indifferent:** unremarkable, average
253. **a strumpet:** because no man can rely on her continued favor

nant sometimes his replies are! a happiness that often
madness hits on, which reason and sanity could not so
prosperously be delivered of. I will leave him and sud-
denly contrive the means of meeting between him and
my daughter.—My honorable lord, I will most humbly 230
take my leave of you.

*Ham.* You cannot, sir, take from me anything that I
will more willingly part withal—except my life, except my
life, except my life.

Enter *Rosencrantz* and *Guildenstern*.

*Pol.* Fare you well, my lord.                                   235
*Ham.* These tedious old fools!
*Pol.* You go to seek the Lord Hamlet. There he is.
*Ros.* [*To Polonius*] God save you, sir!

*Exit* [*Polonius*].

*Guil.* My honored lord!
*Ros.* My most dear lord!                                        240
*Ham.* My excellent good friends! How dost thou,
Guildenstern? Ah, Rosencrantz! Good lads, how do ye
both?
*Ros.* As the indifferent children of the earth.
*Guil.* Happy in that we are not over-happy.                     245
On Fortune's cap we are not the very button.
*Ham.* Nor the soles of her shoe?
*Ros.* Neither, my lord.
*Ham.* Then you live about her waist, or in the middle
of her favors?                                                   250
*Guil.* Faith, her privates we.
*Ham.* In the secret parts of Fortune? O, most true! she
is a strumpet. What news?

262. **goodly**: roomy

279-80. **beggars bodies . . . beggars' shadows**: if ambition is but a "shadow's shadow," then beggars, who are free from ambition, are the substantial humans, while kings and heroes, ruled by ambition, are but shadows.

281. **fay**: faith

282. **wait upon**: accompany, though Hamlet chooses to interpret the words literally

283. **matter**: thing; **sort**: classify

*Ros.* None, my lord, but that the world's grown honest.

*Ham.* Then is doomsday near! But your news is not 255
true. Let me question more in particular. What have you,
my good friends, deserved at the hands of Fortune that
she sends you to prison hither?

*Guil.* Prison, my lord?

*Ham.* Denmark's a prison. 260

*Ros.* Then is the world one.

*Ham.* A goodly one; in which there are many confines,
wards, and dungeons, Denmark being one o' the worst.

*Ros.* We think not so, my lord.

*Ham.* Why, then 'tis none to you, for there is nothing 265
either good or bad but thinking makes it so. To me it is a
prison.

*Ros.* Why, then your ambition makes it one. 'Tis too
narrow for your mind.

*Ham.* O God, I could be bounded in a nutshell and 270
count myself a king of infinite space, were it not that I
have bad dreams.

*Guil.* Which dreams indeed are ambition; for the very
substance of the ambitious is merely the shadow of a
dream. 275

*Ham.* A dream itself is but a shadow.

*Ros.* Truly, and I hold ambition of so airy and light a
quality that it is but a shadow's shadow.

*Ham.* Then are our beggars bodies, and our monarchs
and outstretched heroes the beggars' shadows. Shall we 280
to the court? for, by my fay, I cannot reason.

*Both.* We'll wait upon you.

*Ham.* No such matter! I will not sort you with the rest
of my servants; for, to speak to you like an honest man, I

285-86. **dreadfully attended:** possibly a double meaning is intended: "poorly served" and "accompanied by horrors"; **in the beaten way of friendship:** that is, as old friends, speak frankly.

289-90. **too dear a halfpenny:** not worth a halfpenny

291. **justly:** honestly

296. **color:** conceal

300-1. **the consonancy of our youth:** the congeniality established in our youth

302. **dear:** important; see **dearest** at I. ii. 191.

303. **even:** honest

306. **of:** on

309-10. **prevent your discovery:** forestall disclosure of your real motive

310-11. **your secrecy . . . moult no feather:** your promise of secrecy be undamaged

312. **mirth:** ability to be gay

314-15. **a sterile promontory:** a barren headland (overhanging eternity)

am most dreadfully attended. But in the beaten way of 285
friendship, what make you at Elsinore?

*Ros.* To visit you, my lord; no other occasion.

*Ham.* Beggar that I am, I am even poor in thanks; but
I thank you; and sure, dear friends, my thanks are too
dear a halfpenny. Were you not sent for? Is it your own 290
inclining? Is it a free visitation? Come, deal justly with
me. Come, come! Nay, speak.

*Guil.* What should we say, my lord?

*Ham.* Why, anything, but to the purpose. You were
sent for, and there is a kind of confession in your looks, 295
which your modesties have not craft enough to color. I
know the good King and Queen have sent for you.

*Ros.* To what end, my lord?

*Ham.* That you must teach me. But let me conjure
you by the rights of our fellowship, by the consonancy of 300
our youth, by the obligation of our ever-preserved love,
and by what more dear a better proposer could charge
you withal, be even and direct with me, whether you
were sent for or no.

*Ros.* [*Aside to Guildenstern*] What say you?          305

*Ham.* [*Aside*] Nay then, I have an eye of you. If you
love me, hold not off.

*Guil.* My lord, we were sent for.

*Ham.* I will tell you why, so shall my anticipation prevent your discovery, and your secrecy to the King and 310
Queen moult no feather. I have of late—but wherefore I
know not—lost all my mirth, forgone all custom of exer-
cises; and indeed, it goes so heavily with my disposition
that this goodly frame, the earth, seems to me a sterile
promontory; this most excellent canopy, the air, look you, 315

317. **fretted with golden fire**: decorated with stars like the golden fretwork of a ceiling

320. **express**: exact, precise

323. **quintessence**: concentrated essence

330. **what lenten entertainment**: what a miserable reception

331. **coted**: passed by

335. **foil and target**: sword and shield

336. **the humorous man shall end his part in peace**: the man who impersonates a particular "humor" (as Jaques in *As You Like It* personifies the humor of melancholy) shall speak his part without interruption.

337. **tickle o' the sere**: easy on the trigger; **sere** means the catch in a gunlock.

338-39. **the lady . . . halt for't**: the lady will be allowed to talk as much as she wishes, lest the meter of her speeches be marred.

342. **Their residence**: that is, their residence in the city

344. **inhibition**: restraint

344-45. **the late innovation**: the new popularity of acting companies of boys, as described at ll. 353-54.

this brave o'erhanging firmament, this majestical roof
fretted with golden fire—why, it appeareth no other thing
to me than a foul and pestilent congregation of vapors.
What a piece of work is a man! how noble in reason! how
infinite in faculties! in form and moving how express and   320
admirable! in action how like an angel! in apprehension
how like a god! the beauty of the world, the paragon of
animals! And yet to me what is this quintessence of dust?
Man delights not me—no, nor woman neither, though by
your smiling you seem to say so.                            325

*Ros.* My lord, there was no such stuff in my thoughts.

*Ham.* Why did you laugh then, when I said "Man delights not me"?

*Ros.* To think, my lord, if you delight not in man,
what lenten entertainment the players shall receive from   330
you. We coted them on the way, and hither are they
coming to offer you service.

*Ham.* He that plays the king shall be welcome—his
Majesty shall have tribute of me; the adventurous knight
shall use his foil and target; the lover shall not sigh gratis; 335
the humorous man shall end his part in peace; the clown
shall make those laugh whose lungs are tickle o' the sere;
and the lady shall say her mind freely, or the blank verse
shall halt for't. What players are they?

*Ros.* Even those you were wont to take such delight   340
in, the tragedians of the city.

*Ham.* How chances it they travel? Their residence,
both in reputation and profit, was better both ways.

*Ros.* I think their inhibition comes by the means of the
late innovation.                                            345

*Ham.* Do they hold the same estimation they did
when I was in the city? Are they so followed?

351. **eyrie:** brood; **eyases:** unfledged hawks

351-52. **cry out on the top of question:** declaim in shrill voices with more oratory than the matter requires; **tyrannically:** immoderately, extravagantly

353-54. **berattle the common stages:** deride public theatres. Plays especially written for the boys ridiculed the public playhouses so severely that they became temporarily unfashionable.

358-59. **escoted:** supported; **pursue the quality no longer than they can sing:** follow the acting profession only until their voices change

361. **if their means are no better:** if they cannot support themselves in a better way; **their writers:** that is, the writers who supplied them with satirical material

365. **tarre:** incite

366-67. **There was . . . in the question:** the controversy had excited so much interest that no producer would buy plays which did not harp on this theme.

371. **carry it away:** come off the winners

372-73. **Hercules and his load too:** a reference to Hercules' support of the globe on his shoulders for Atlas, which was pictured on the sign of the Globe playhouse. In other words, Shakespeare's own company suffered from the competition of the child players.

375. **mows:** mouths, grimaces

377. **picture in little:** miniature

*Ros.* No indeed are they not.

*Ham.* How comes it? Do they grow rusty?

*Ros.* Nay, their endeavor keeps in the wonted pace; 350
but there is, sir, an eyrie of children, little eyases, that cry
out on the top of question and are most tyrannically
clapped for't. These are now the fashion, and so berattle
the common stages (so they call them) that many wearing rapiers are afraid of goosequills and dare scarce come 355
thither.

*Ham.* What, are they children? Who maintains 'em?
How are they escoted? Will they pursue the quality no
longer than they can sing? Will they not say afterwards,
if they should grow themselves to common players (as it 360
is most like, if their means are no better), their writers do
them wrong to make them exclaim against their own succession?

*Ros.* Faith, there has been much to do on both sides;
and the nation holds it no sin to tarre them to controversy. 365
There was, for a while, no money bid for argument unless
the poet and the player went to cuffs in the question.

*Ham.* Is't possible?

*Guil.* O, there has been much throwing about of
brains. 370

*Ham.* Do the boys carry it away?

*Ros.* Ay, that they do, my lord—Hercules and his load
too.

*Ham.* It is not very strange; for my uncle is King of
Denmark, and those that would make mows at him while 375
my father lived give twenty, forty, fifty, a hundred ducats
apiece for his picture in little. 'Sblood, there is something
in this more than natural, if philosophy could find it out.

381. **appurtenance**: accessory

382. **comply with you**: display courteous formalities with you; **garb**: way

383. **extent**: extension of courtesy

388-89. **I am but mad north-north-west. When the wind is southerly I know a hawk from a handsaw**: According to Timothy Bright's *Treatise of Melancholy* (1586), the condition of the melancholic's mood varied with the winds and would be worst when the wind came from the north. Hamlet is saying in veiled terms that his madness is assumed when it suits his purpose. To "know a hawk from a handsaw" expresses a proverbial idea. **Handsaw** may be a quibble on "heronshaw," an old form of "heron," but the general sense of the phrase is merely that he can distinguish between unlike objects; he is not such a fool as he looks.

393. **clouts**: clothes

394. **Happily**: perhaps; see I. i. 147.

400-1. **Roscius**: a famous actor of Cicero's time. This passage is Hamlet's way of saying that Polonius' news is old; he already knows of the actors' arrival.

*Flourish for the Players.*

*Guil.* There are the players.

*Ham.* Gentlemen, you are welcome to Elsinore. Your 380
hands, come! The appurtenance of welcome is fashion
and ceremony. Let me comply with you in this garb, lest
my extent to the players (which I tell you must show fairly outwards) should more appear like entertainment than
yours. You are welcome. But my uncle-father and aunt- 385
mother are deceived.

*Guil.* In what, my dear lord?

*Ham.* I am but mad north-north-west. When the wind
is southerly I know a hawk from a handsaw.

*Enter Polonius.*

*Pol.* Well be with you, gentlemen! 390

*Ham.* Hark you, Guildenstern—and you too—at each
ear a hearer! That great baby you see there is not yet out
of his swaddling clouts.

*Ros.* Happily he's the second time come to them; for
they say an old man is twice a child. 395

*Ham.* I will prophesy he comes to tell me of the players. Mark it.—You say right, sir; a Monday morning; 'twas
so indeed.

*Pol.* My lord, I have news to tell you.

*Ham.* My lord, I have news to tell you: when Roscius 400
was an actor in Rome—

*Pol.* The actors are come hither, my lord.

*Ham.* Buzz, buzz!

405. **Then came each actor on his ass:** possibly a line from a song, with which Hamlet ridicules Polonius' last words

409. **scene individable, or poem unlimited:** plays that preserve unity in time and place, according to classical prescription, contrasted with others that violate such unity; **Seneca:** a Roman dramatist, whose tragedies were imitated by Elizabethan playwrights

410-11. **Plautus:** a Roman writer of farcical comedies; **For the law of writ and the liberty:** for either the observation of rules of composition or freedom in writing

412. **Jephthah:** Hamlet goes on to quote a late sixteenth-century ballad about Jephthah's sacrifice of his daughter. The Biblical source is Judges 11:34-39.

417. **passing:** exceedingly

428. **row:** stanza; **pious:** so-called because of its scriptural subject

*Pol.* Upon my honor—

*Ham.* Then came each actor on his ass—   405

*Pol.* The best actors in the world, either for tragedy, comedy, history, pastoral, pastoral-comical, historical-pastoral, tragical-historical, tragical-comical-historical-pastoral; scene individable, or poem unlimited. Seneca cannot be too heavy, nor Plautus too light. For the law of   410 writ and the liberty, these are the only men.

*Ham.* O Jephthah, judge of Israel, what a treasure hadst thou!

*Pol.* What a treasure had he, my lord?

*Ham.* Why,   415

> *One fair daughter, and no more,*
> *The which he loved passing well.*

*Pol.* [*Aside*] Still on my daughter.

*Ham.* Am I not i' the right, old Jephthah?

*Pol.* If you call me Jephthah, my lord, I have a daugh-   420 ter that I love passing well.

*Ham.* Nay, that follows not.

*Pol.* What follows then, my lord?

*Ham.* Why,

> *As by lot, God wot,*   425

and then, you know,

> *It came to pass, as most like it was.*

The first row of the pious chanson will show you more; for look where my abridgment comes.

432. **valanced**: fringed; that is, he has a beard.

433-34. **young lady and mistress**: the boy actor addressed was the female lead. No company of players included women in this period; Hamlet is being jocular.

435. **a chopine**: a shoe with a very thick sole, originally very fashionable in Italy and also worn in England in the seventeenth century

436-37. **a piece of uncurrent gold . . . cracked within the ring**: coins were not negotiable when cracked through the circle which surrounded the image of the ruling sovereign. Hamlet hopes the boy's voice has not begun to change.

438. **French falconers**: the French were noted for their skill at falconry.

439. **straight**: immediately

440. **quality**: profession; as before at II. ii. 358.

444-45. **caviary to the general**: too choice for the average taste

446. **cried in the top of**: exceeded

449. **sallets**: salads, which were usually highly seasoned; hence, spicy bits

451. **honest**: chaste

452. **more handsome than fine**: more elegant than gaudy

453. **Æneas**: hero of Virgil's *Æneid,* which describes his adventures after the Trojan War

454. **Dido**: queen of Carthage

455. **Priam**: king of Troy

457. **Pyrrhus**: son of the Greek hero Achilles; **Hyrcanian beast**: tiger. Hyrcania: a region in Asia

54

Enter four or five *Players*.

You are welcome, masters; welcome, all.—I am glad to 430
see thee well.—Welcome, good friends.—O, my old friend?
Why, thy face is valanced since I saw thee last. Com'st
thou to beard me in Denmark?—What, my young lady
and mistress? By'r Lady, your ladyship is nearer to heaven
than when I saw you last by the altitude of a chopine. 435
Pray God your voice, like a piece of uncurrent gold, be
not cracked within the ring.—Masters, you are all welcome. We'll e'en to't like French falconers, fly at anything
we see. We'll have a speech straight. Come, give us a
taste of your quality. Come, a passionate speech. 440

*1. Play.* What speech, my good lord?

*Ham.* I heard thee speak me a speech once, but it was
never acted; or if it was, not above once; for the play, I
remember, pleased not the million, 'twas caviary to the
general; but it was (as I received it, and others, whose 445
judgments in such matters cried in the top of mine) an
excellent play, well digested in the scenes, set down with
as much modesty as cunning. I remember one said there
were no sallets in the lines to make the matter savory, nor
no matter in the phrase that might indict the author of 450
affectation; but called it an honest method, as wholesome
as sweet, and by very much more handsome than fine.
One speech in it I chiefly loved. 'Twas Æneas' tale to
Dido, and thereabout of it especially where he speaks of
Priam's slaughter. If it live in your memory, begin at this 455
line—let me see, let me see:

*The rugged Pyrrhus, like the Hyrcanian beast—*

Pyrrhus and Hecuba.
From Ovid, *Metamorphoses* (1565).

459. **sable arms:** the black heraldic device displayed on his shield

461. **horse:** the wooden horse with which the Greeks tricked the Trojans

464. **gules:** the heraldic word for red; **tricked:** decorated; another heraldic term

467. **tyrannous:** fierce

469. **o'ersized:** overglazed

470. **like carbuncles:** that is, glowing red

478. **Repugnant:** disobedient

480. **fell:** deadly

481. **Ilium:** Troy's "topless towers"; that is, the fortified battlements

483. **his:** its

'Tis not so; it begins with Pyrrhus:

> *The rugged Pyrrhus, he whose sable arms,*
> *Black as his purpose, did the night resemble*                460
> *When he lay couched in the ominous horse,*
> *Hath now this dread and black complexion smeared*
> *With heraldry more dismal. Head to foot*
> *Now is he total gules, horridly tricked*
> *With blood of fathers, mothers, daughters, sons,*            465
> *Baked and impasted with the parching streets,*
> *That lend a tyrannous and a damned light*
> *To their lord's murder. Roasted in wrath and fire,*
> *And thus o'ersized with coagulate gore,*
> *With eyes like carbuncles, the hellish Pyrrhus*             470
> *Old grandsire Priam seeks.*

So, proceed you.
   *Pol.* Fore God, my lord, well spoken, with good accent
and good discretion.

> *1. Play.*                          *Anon he finds him,*      475
> *Striking too short at Greeks. His antique sword,*
> *Rebellious to his arm, lies where it falls,*
> *Repugnant to command. Unequal matched,*
> *Pyrrhus at Priam drives, in rage strikes wide;*
> *But with the whiff and wind of his fell sword*              480
> *The unnerved father falls. Then senseless Ilium,*
> *Seeming to feel this blow, with flaming top*
> *Stoops to his base, and with a hideous crash*
> *Takes prisoner Pyrrhus' ear. For lo! his sword,*
> *Which was declining on the milky head*                      485
> *Of reverend Priam, seemed i' the air to stick.*

Mars.
From Cartari, *Imagini delli Dei de gl'Antichi* (1674).

490. **against:** just before; see I. i. 173.

491. **rack:** cloud formation

492. **the orb below:** the earth

494. **region:** the upper air

496. **the Cyclops:** the giants who assisted Vulcan, the blacksmith for the other gods, according to Greek mythology

497. **Mars:** the Roman god of war; **for proof eterne:** for eternal trial

502. **fellies:** sections forming a wheel's rim; **wheel:** Fortune, personified as a woman, was often pictured as controlling human destinies by the turn of her great wheel.

503. **nave:** hub

507. **jig:** a brief farce or "turn"

508. **Hecuba:** wife of Priam; see II. ii. 455.

509. **mobled:** muffled

514. **bisson rheum:** blinding tears; **clout:** cloth; see II. ii. 393.

56

So, as a painted tyrant, Pyrrhus stood,
And, like a neutral to his will and matter,
Did nothing.
But, as we often see, against some storm,                    490
A silence in the heavens, the rack stand still,
The bold winds speechless, and the orb below
As hush as death—anon the dreadful thunder
Doth rend the region; so, after Pyrrhus' pause,
Aroused vengeance sets him new awork;                    495
And never did the Cyclops' hammers fall
On Mars's armor, forged for proof eterne,
With less remorse than Pyrrhus' bleeding sword
Now falls on Priam.
Out, out, thou strumpet Fortune! All you gods,                    500
In general synod take away her power;
Break all the spokes and fellies from her wheel,
And bowl the round nave down the hill of heaven,
As low as to the fiends!

*Pol.* This is too long.                    505
*Ham.* It shall to the barber's, with your beard.—Prithee
say on. He's for a jig or a tale of bawdry, or he sleeps. Say
on; come to Hecuba.

*1. Play.* But who, O who, had seen the mobled queen—

*Ham.* "The mobled queen"?                    510
*Pol.* That's good! "Mobled queen" is good.

*1. Play.* Run barefoot up and down, threat'ning the
        flames
With bisson rheum; a clout upon that head
Where late the diadem stood, and for a robe,                    515

516. **all o'erteemed:** completely exhausted from bearing children

519. **'Gainst Fortune's state would treason have pronounced:** that is, would have railed against Fortune's control of human affairs

525. **milch:** wet with tears

526. **passion:** deep emotion

527. **whe'r:** whether

528. **in's:** in his

530-31. **bestowed:** accommodated

533. **you were better have:** you would be better to have

536. **bodykins:** little body (used affectionately)

*About her lank and all o'erteemed loins,*
*A blanket, in the alarm of fear caught up—*
*Who this had seen, with tongue in venom steeped*
*'Gainst Fortune's state would treason have pronounced.*
*But if the gods themselves did see her then,* 520
*When she saw Pyrrhus make malicious sport*
*In mincing with his sword her husband's limbs,*
*The instant burst of clamor that she made*
*(Unless things mortal move them not at all)*
*Would have made milch the burning eyes of heaven* 525
*And passion in the gods.*

*Pol.* Look, whe'r he has not turned his color, and has tears in's eyes. Prithee no more!

*Ham.* 'Tis well. I'll have thee speak out the rest of this soon.—Good my lord, will you see the players well be- 530 stowed? Do you hear? Let them be well used; for they are the abstract and brief chronicles of the time. After your death you were better have a bad epitaph than their ill report while you live.

*Pol.* My lord, I will use them according to their desert. 535

*Ham.* God's bodykins, man, much better! Use every man after his desert, and who should scape whipping? Use them after your own honor and dignity. The less they deserve, the more merit is in your bounty. Take them in. 540

*Pol.* Come, sirs.

*Ham.* Follow him, friends. We'll hear a play tomorrow.
        *Exeunt Polonius and Players [except the First].*
Dost thou hear me, old friend? Can you play "The Murder of Gonzago"?

559. **Could force his soul so to his own conceit:** could so arouse his own emotion by the imaginative creation of his role

560. **from her working: her** refers to "conceit," that is, the player's portrayal of his role

570. **Make mad the guilty:** madden spectators whose consciences were troubled by guilt; **appal the free:** overcome the innocent with fear

571. **Confound:** confuse; **amaze:** astound

574. **dull and muddy-mettled:** abject and cowardly; **peak:** mope

575. **John-a-dreams:** a proverbial name for a habitual dreamer; **unpregnant of my cause:** not stirred to action by my cause

*1. Play.* Ay, my lord.                                                    545

*Ham.* We'll ha't tomorrow night. You could, for a
need, study a speech of some dozen or sixteen lines which
I would set down and insert in't, could you not?

*1. Play.* Ay, my lord.

*Ham.* Very well. Follow that lord—and look you mock   550
him not. [*Exit First Player.*] My good friends, I'll leave
you till night. You are welcome to Elsinore.

*Ros.* Good my lord!

*Ham.* Ay, so, God be wi' ye!

                    *Exeunt* [*Rosencrantz and Guildenstern*].
                              Now I am alone.              555
O, what a rogue and peasant slave am I!
Is it not monstrous that this player here,
But in a fiction, in a dream of passion,
Could force his soul so to his own conceit
That, from her working, all his visage wanned,          560
Tears in his eyes, distraction in's aspect,
A broken voice, and his whole function suiting
With forms to his conceit? And all for nothing!
For Hecuba!
What's Hecuba to him, or he to Hecuba,                   565
That he should weep for her? What would he do,
Had he the motive and the cue for passion
That I have? He would drown the stage with tears
And cleave the general ear with horrid speech;
Make mad the guilty and appal the free,                  570
Confound the ignorant, and amaze indeed
The very faculties of eyes and ears.
Yet I,
A dull and muddy-mettled rascal, peak
Like John-a-dreams, unpregnant of my cause,             575

578. **defeat:** destruction

579. **pate:** head

583. **'Swounds:** God's wounds, also abbreviated "Zounds"

586. **region kites:** falcon-like birds of the air; see II. ii. 494.

588. **kindless:** unnatural. Killing his brother and marrying his brother's wife were both unnatural acts.

593. **unpack:** relieve

594. **drab:** disreputable woman

595. **scullion:** kitchen servant

598. **cunning:** skill of presentation

599. **presently:** at once

605. **tent:** probe

And can say nothing! No, not for a king,
Upon whose property and most dear life
A damned defeat was made. Am I a coward?
Who calls me villain? breaks my pate across?
Plucks off my beard and blows it in my face?     580
Tweaks me by the nose? gives me the lie i' the throat
As deep as to the lungs? Who does me this, ha?
'Swounds, I should take it! for it cannot be
But I am pigeon-livered and lack gall
To make oppression bitter, or ere this     585
I should have fatted all the region kites
With this slave's offal. Bloody, bawdy villain!
Remorseless, treacherous, lecherous, kindless villain!
O, vengeance!
Why, what an ass am I! This is most brave,     590
That I, the son of a dear father murdered,
Prompted to my revenge by heaven and hell,
Must (like a whore) unpack my heart with words
And fall a-cursing like a very drab,
A scullion!     595
Fie upon't! foh! About, my brain! I have heard
That guilty creatures, sitting at a play,
Have by the very cunning of the scene
Been struck so to the soul that presently
They have proclaimed their malefactions;     600
For murder, though it have no tongue, will speak
With most miraculous organ. I'll have these players
Play something like the murder of my father
Before mine uncle. I'll observe his looks,
I'll tent him to the quick; if he but blench,     605
I know my course. The spirit that I have seen
May be a devil; and the devil hath power

610. **spirits:** moods
611. **Abuses:** deceives; see I. [v.] 44.
612. **relative:** closely related, relevant

T' assume a pleasing shape; yea, and perhaps
Out of my weakness and my melancholy,
As he is very potent with such spirits,                    610
Abuses me to damn me. I'll have grounds
More relative than this. The play's the thing
Wherein I'll catch the conscience of the King.

*Exit.*

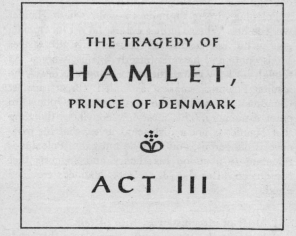

THE TRAGEDY OF

# HAMLET,
PRINCE OF DENMARK

## ACT III

**III.** [i.] Rosencrantz and Guildenstern report to Claudius, but they are able to reveal little except Hamlet's order for a play to be put on that night. Claudius dispatches them to seek Hamlet and encourage this diversion.

Polonius directs Ophelia to walk where Hamlet will see her. When Hamlet enters, he greets Ophelia gently, but her gesture of returning his gifts strikes a false note and he rails bitterly against women. As though he knows that they are being overheard, he insults Polonius, makes a veiled threat against Claudius' life, and as he leaves, urges Ophelia to enter a nunnery. This interview convinces the King that Hamlet is not a distracted lover, that his presence is dangerous, and that he must die. Polonius is reluctant to abandon his theory and suggests that the Queen, after the play, probe Hamlet's troubled mind.

<hr/>

1. **drift of circumstance:** turn of talk

2. **puts on this confusion:** pretends to this madness

14-5. **Niggard of question, but of our demands/ Most free in his reply:** sparing in his attempts at conversation but ready in answering our questions

16. **assay:** assail with argument

# ACT III

[Scene I. Elsinore. A room in the Castle.]

Enter *King, Queen, Polonius, Ophelia, Rosencrantz, Guildenstern,* and *Lords.*

*King.* And can you by no drift of circumstance
Get from him why he puts on this confusion,
Grating so harshly all his days of quiet
With turbulent and dangerous lunacy?

*Ros.* He does confess he feels himself distracted,     5
But from what cause he will by no means speak.

*Guil.* Nor do we find him forward to be sounded,
But with a crafty madness keeps aloof
When we would bring him on to some confession
Of his true state.                                        10

*Queen.*          Did he receive you well?

*Ros.* Most like a gentleman.

*Guil.* But with much forcing of his disposition.

*Ros.* Niggard of question, but of our demands
Most free in his reply.                                   15

*Queen.*               Did you assay him
To any pastime?

*Ros.* Madam, it so fell out that certain players

19. **o'erraught:** reached and passed
27. **content:** please
33. **closely:** secretly
35. **Affront:** meet face to face
36. **espials:** spies

We o'erraught on the way. Of these we told him,
And there did seem in him a kind of joy                    20
To hear of it. They are here about the court,
And, as I think, they have already order
This night to play before him.
   *Pol.*               'Tis most true;
And he beseeched me to entreat your Majesties              25
To hear and see the matter.
   *King.* With all my heart, and it doth much content me
To hear him so inclined.
Good gentlemen, give him a further edge
And drive his purpose on to these delights.               30
   *Ros.* We shall, my lord.
              *Exeunt Rosencrantz and Guildenstern.*
   *King.*           Sweet Gertrude, leave us too;
For we have closely sent for Hamlet hither,
That he, as 'twere by accident, may here
Affront Ophelia.                                          35
Her father and myself (lawful espials)
Will so bestow ourselves that, seeing unseen,
We may of their encounter frankly judge
And gather by him, as he is behaved,
If't be the affliction of his love, or no,                40
That thus he suffers for.
   *Queen.*         I shall obey you;
And for your part, Ophelia, I do wish
That your good beauties be the happy cause
Of Hamlet's wildness. So shall I hope your virtues        45
Will bring him to his wonted way again,
To both your honors.
   *Oph.*          Madam, I wish it may.
                   *[Exit Queen.]*

52-3. **color/ Your loneliness:** make your solitude appear more natural

60. **to:** compared with

73. **rub:** obstacle, catch

75. **shuffled off this mortal coil:** this can mean either "cast off the yoke of human trouble," or "removed the encumbrance of the flesh."

*Pol.* Ophelia, walk you here.—Gracious, so please you,
We will bestow ourselves.—[*To Ophelia*] Read on this 50
    book,
That show of such an exercise may color
Your loneliness.—We are oft to blame in this,
'Tis too much proved, that with devotion's visage
And pious action we do sugar o'er 55
The devil himself.

*King.* [*Aside*] O, 'tis too true!
How smart a lash that speech doth give my conscience!
The harlot's cheek, beautied with plast'ring art,
Is not more ugly to the thing that helps it 60
Than is my deed to my most painted word.
O heavy burden!

*Pol.* I hear him coming. Let's withdraw, my lord.
                    *Exeunt* [*King and Polonius*].


Enter *Hamlet*.


*Ham.* To be, or not to be, that is the question:
Whether 'tis nobler in the mind to suffer 65
The slings and arrows of outrageous fortune
Or to take arms against a sea of troubles,
And by opposing end them. To die—to sleep—
No more; and by a sleep to say we end
The heartache, and the thousand natural shocks 70
That flesh is heir to. 'Tis a consummation
Devoutly to be wished. To die—to sleep.
To sleep—perchance to dream: ay, there's the rub!
For in that sleep of death what dreams may come
When we have shuffled off this mortal coil, 75
Must give us pause. There's the respect

77. **makes calamity of so long life:** makes calamity last so long; that is, causes us to live out a long life of calamity

79. **contumely:** humiliation

81. **office:** officials in general

83. **quietus:** release; from the legal phrase *Quietus est,* "He is quit"

84. **bare bodkin:** a **bodkin** was a dagger. **Bare** may mean "mere" or "unsheathed"; **fardels:** bundles, burdens.

87. **undiscovered:** unexplored; **bourn:** boundary

92. **native hue of resolution:** the natural ruddy complexion of one resolved on an action

95. **With this regard:** because of this consideration

96. **Soft you:** hush.

That makes calamity of so long life.
For who would bear the whips and scorns of time,
The oppressor's wrong, the proud man's contumely,
The pangs of despised love, the law's delay,                    80
The insolence of office, and the spurns
That patient merit of the unworthy takes,
When he himself might his quietus make
With a bare bodkin? Who would these fardels bear,
To grunt and sweat under a weary life,                          85
But that the dread of something after death—
The undiscovered country, from whose bourn
No traveller returns—puzzles the will,
And makes us rather bear those ills we have
Than fly to others that we know not of?                         90
Thus conscience does make cowards of us all,
And thus the native hue of resolution
Is sicklied o'er with the pale cast of thought,
And enterprises of great pith and moment
With this regard their currents turn awry                       95
And lose the name of action.—Soft you now!
The fair Ophelia!—Nymph, in thy orisons
Be all my sins rememb'red.
   *Oph.*              Good my lord,
How does your honor for this many a day?                        100
   *Ham.* I humbly thank you; well, well, well.
   *Oph.* My lord, I have remembrances of yours
That I have longed long to redeliver.
I pray you, now receive them.
   *Ham.*             No, not I!                      105
I never gave you aught.
   *Oph.* My honored lord, you know right well you did,
And with them words of so sweet breath composed

113. **honest:** chaste (see II. ii. 451), as well as the more obvious meaning

124. **sometime:** formerly

127-28. **virtue cannot so inoculate our old stock but we shall relish of it:** virtue cannot be grafted upon old stock so as to change its characteristic wickedness.

132. **indifferent honest:** reasonably virtuous; see II. ii. 244.

As made the things more rich. Their perfume lost,
Take these again; for to the noble mind                        110
Rich gifts wax poor when givers prove unkind.
There, my lord.
*Ham.* Ha, ha! Are you honest?
*Oph.* My lord?
*Ham.* Are you fair?                                            115
*Oph.* What means your lordship?
*Ham.* That if you be honest and fair, your honesty
should admit no discourse to your beauty.
*Oph.* Could beauty, my lord, have better commerce
than with honesty?                                             120
*Ham.* Ay, truly; for the power of beauty will sooner
transform honesty from what it is to a bawd than the
force of honesty can translate beauty into his likeness.
This was sometime a paradox, but now the time gives it
proof. I did love you once.                                    125
*Oph.* Indeed, my lord, you made me believe so.
*Ham.* You should not have believed me; for virtue cannot so inoculate our old stock but we shall relish of it. I
loved you not.
*Oph.* I was the more deceived.                                130
*Ham.* Get thee to a nunnery! Why wouldst thou be a
breeder of sinners? I am myself indifferent honest, but yet
I could accuse me of such things that it were better my
mother had not borne me. I am very proud, revengeful,
ambitious; with more offenses at my beck than I have     135
thoughts to put them in, imagination to give them shape,
or time to act them in. What should such fellows as I do,
crawling between earth and heaven? We are arrant
knaves all; believe none of us. Go thy ways to a nunnery.
Where's your father?                                           140

149. **monsters:** men deformed by horns, the proverbial picture of a husband whose wife has betrayed him

154–56. **you nickname God's creatures and make your wantonness your ignorance:** you name things according to your whim and then pretend that your willfulness is mere ignorance.

156. **on't:** of it; see I. i. 66.

157. **mo:** (adj., adv., and noun) from Anglo-Saxon **ma,** more, further, other greater number; **more** derives from the same Anglo-Saxon word but is a different word; i.e., **mo** is not a spelling of **more,** and the latter word has a wider variety of meanings.

162. **The expectancy and rose of the fair state:** the heir who is expected to be the country's chief beauty when he assumes its government

163. **mould of form:** model of behavior

169. **blown:** full-blown

170. **ecstasy:** madness; see II. [i.] 113.

*Oph.* At home, my lord.

*Ham.* Let the doors be shut upon him, that he may play the fool nowhere but in's own house. Farewell.

*Oph.* O, help him, you sweet heavens!

*Ham.* If thou dost marry, I'll give thee this plague for 145 thy dowry: be thou as chaste as ice, as pure as snow, thou shalt not escape calumny. Get thee to a nunnery. Go, farewell. Or if thou wilt needs marry, marry a fool; for wise men know well enough what monsters you make of them. To a nunnery, go; and quickly too. Farewell. 150

*Oph.* O heavenly powers, restore him!

*Ham.* I have heard of your paintings too, well enough. God hath given you one face, and you make yourselves another. You jig, you amble, and you lisp; you nickname God's creatures and make your wantonness your igno- 155 rance. Go to, I'll no more on't! it hath made me mad. I say, we will have no mo marriages. Those that are married already—all but one—shall live; the rest shall keep as they are. To a nunnery, go. *Exit.*

*Oph.* O, what a noble mind is here o'erthrown! 160
The courtier's, soldier's, scholar's, eye, tongue, sword,
The expectancy and rose of the fair state,
The glass of fashion and the mould of form,
The observed of all observers—quite, quite down!
And I, of ladies most deject and wretched, 165
That sucked the honey of his music vows,
Now see that noble and most sovereign reason,
Like sweet bells jangled, out of tune and harsh;
That unmatched form and feature of blown youth
Blasted with ecstasy. O, woe is me 170
T' have seen what I have seen, see what I see!

172. **affections**: emotions
176. **disclose**: disclosure of the hatch; that is, out-come
183. **something-settled**: somewhat fixed
184. **still**: ever; see I. [v.] 214.
193. **round**: blunt; see II. ii. 149.
195. **find him not**: does not find out his trouble

Enter *King* and *Polonius*.

*King.* Love? his affections do not that way tend;
Nor what he spake, though it lacked form a little,
Was not like madness. There's something in his soul
O'er which his melancholy sits on brood;        175
And I do doubt the hatch and the disclose
Will be some danger; which for to prevent,
I have in quick determination
Thus set it down: he shall with speed to England
For the demand of our neglected tribute.        180
Haply the seas, and countries different,
With variable objects, shall expel
This something-settled matter in his heart,
Whereon his brains still beating puts him thus
From fashion of himself. What think you on't?        185
    *Pol.* It shall do well. But yet do I believe
The origin and commencement of his grief
Sprung from neglected love.—How now, Ophelia?
You need not tell us what Lord Hamlet said,
We heard it all.—My lord, do as you please;        190
But if you hold it fit, after the play
Let his queen mother all alone entreat him
To show his grief. Let her be round with him;
And I'll be placed, so please you, in the ear
Of all their conference. If she find him not,        195
To England send him; or confine him where
Your wisdom best shall think.
    *King.*                It shall be so.
Madness in great ones must not unwatched go.
                                *Exeunt.*

III. [ii.] Hamlet instructs the players in acting techniques and privately sets Horatio to watch the King's reaction to the play. He himself chooses to sit by Ophelia and embarrass her with coarse jests interspersed with a running commentary designed to torture Claudius.

The players present a pantomime with a plot similar to the circumstances of Claudius' murder of Hamlet's father and the winning of his wife. Perturbed by the dialogue of the poisoning scene, Claudius can stand no more and leaves precipitately, followed by all present except Hamlet and Horatio. Rosencrantz and Guildenstern return to announce the King's anger and the Queen's desire to see Hamlet at once. As he leaves, Hamlet appears resolved to kill Claudius that night.

▪▪▪▪▪▪▪▪▪▪▪▪▪▪▪▪▪▪▪▪▪▪▪▪▪▪▪▪▪▪

10. **groundlings:** those of the audience who stood in the yard; that is, the lowest class of spectator

11. **capable:** capable of appreciating

13. **Termagant:** a Saracen god who appeared as a fiend in early morality plays; **Herod:** represented in the early drama as violently melodramatic

19. **modesty:** temperance

20. **from:** away from

23. **the very age and body:** the actual image both as to age and conformation

24. **pressure:** impression

24-5. **come tardy off:** inadequately performed; **unskilful:** undiscriminating, ignorant

68

[Scene II. Elsinore. A hall in the Castle.]

Enter *Hamlet* and three of the *Players*.

*Ham.* Speak the speech, I pray you, as I pronounced
it to you, trippingly on the tongue. But if you mouth it,
as many of our players do, I had as lief the town crier
spoke my lines. Nor do not saw the air too much with
your hand, thus, but use all gently; for in the very torrent,    5
tempest, and (as I may say) whirlwind of your passion,
you must acquire and beget a temperance that may give
it smoothness. O, it offends me to the soul to hear a ro-
bustious periwig-pated fellow tear a passion to tatters, to
very rags, to split the ears of the groundlings, who (for    10
the most part) are capable of nothing but inexplicable
dumb shows and noise. I would have such a fellow
whipped for o'erdoing Termagant. It out-herods Herod.
Pray you avoid it.

*Player.* I warrant your honor.    15

*Ham.* Be not too tame neither; but let your own discretion be your tutor. Suit the action to the word, the word
to the action; with this special observance, that you
o'erstep not the modesty of nature: for anything so overdone is from the purpose of playing, whose end, both at    20
the first and now, was and is, to hold, as 'twere, the
mirror up to nature; to show virtue her own feature,
scorn her own image, and the very age and body of the
time his form and pressure. Now this overdone, or come
tardy off, though it make the unskilful laugh, cannot but    25

26. **censure**: judgment; see I. iii. 73.

27. **in your allowance**: that is, you must concede.

29-30. **(not to speak it profanely)**: not intending to offend the deity with what follows

35. **indifferently**: fairly well, see III. [i.] 132.

40. **barren**: stupid

make the judicious grieve; the censure of the which one
must in your allowance o'erweigh a whole theatre of
others. O, there be players that I have seen play, and
heard others praise, and that highly (not to speak it
profanely), that, neither having the accent of Christians,    30
nor the gait of Christian, pagan, nor man, have so strutted
and bellowed that I have thought some of Nature's
journeymen had made men, and not made them well,
they imitated humanity so abominably.

*Player.* I hope we have reformed that indifferently with    35
us, sir.

*Ham.* O, reform it altogether! And let those that play
your clowns speak no more than is set down for them.
For there be of them that will themselves laugh, to set
on some quantity of barren spectators to laugh too,    40
though in the mean time some necessary question of the
play be then to be considered. That's villainous and
shows a most pitiful ambition in the fool that uses it.
Go make you ready.

*Exeunt Players.*


Enter *Polonius, Rosencrantz,* and *Guildenstern.*


How now, my lord? Will the King hear this piece of    45
work?

*Pol.* And the Queen too, and that presently.

*Ham.* Bid the players make haste. (*Exit Polonius.*) Will
you two help to hasten them?

*Both.* We will, my lord.            *Exeunt they two.*    50
*Ham.* What, ho, Horatio!

53. **just**: even; that is, well-balanced

54. **As e'er my conversation coped withal**: as I ever encountered in human intercourse

62. **pregnant**: ready

63. **thrift**: financial success

64. **dear**: valuable; see II. ii. 302.

65. **election**: choice

Enter *Horatio*.

*Hor.* Here, sweet lord, at your service.
*Ham.* Horatio, thou art e'en as just a man
As e'er my conversation coped withal.
*Hor.* O, my dear lord!                                          55
*Ham.*                    Nay, do not think I flatter;
For what advancement may I hope from thee,
That no revenue hast but thy good spirits
To feed and clothe thee? Why should the poor be flat-
    tered?                                                       60
No, let the candied tongue lick absurd pomp,
And crook the pregnant hinges of the knee
Where thrift may follow fawning. Dost thou hear?
Since my dear soul was mistress of her choice
And could of men distinguish, her election               65
Hath sealed thee for herself. For thou hast been
As one, in suff'ring all, that suffers nothing;
A man that Fortune's buffets and rewards
Hast ta'en with equal thanks; and blest are those
Whose blood and judgment are so well commingled        70
That they are not a pipe for Fortune's finger
To sound what stop she please. Give me that man
That is not passion's slave, and I will wear him
In my heart's core, ay, in my heart of heart,
As I do thee. Something too much of this!                75
There is a play tonight before the King.
One scene of it comes near the circumstance,
Which I have told thee, of my father's death.
I prithee, when thou seest that act afoot,

80. **comment:** observation

81. **occulted:** deliberately concealed

85. **stithy:** forge

95. **chameleon's dish:** the chameleon's tongue flicks up insects with such speed that to the observer it appears to have taken in nothing but air.

96. **promise-crammed:** a reference to the King's promise that Hamlet will inherit the throne, a promise that Hamlet implies is empty

97-8. **These words are not mine:** that is, the answer does not fit my question.

"Vulcan's stithy."
From Cartari, *Imagini delli Dei de gl'Antichi* (1674).

Even with the very comment of thy soul     80
Observe my uncle. If his occulted guilt
Do not itself unkennel in one speech,
It is a damned ghost that we have seen,
And my imaginations are as foul
As Vulcan's stithy. Give him heedful note;     85
For I mine eyes will rivet to his face,
And after we will both our judgments join
In censure of his seeming.
    *Hor.*                Well, my lord.
If he steal aught the whilst this play is playing,     90
And scape detecting, I will pay the theft.
*Sound a flourish.* Enter *Trumpets* and *Kettledrums.*
*Danish march.* Enter *King, Queen, Polonius, Ophelia,*
*Rosencrantz, Guildenstern,* and other *Lords* attendant,
    with his [*the King's*] *Guard* carrying torches.

    *Ham.* They are coming to the play: I must be idle.
Get you a place.
    *King.* How fares our cousin Hamlet?
    *Ham.* Excellent, i' faith, of the chameleon's dish: I eat     95
the air, promise-crammed. You cannot feed capons so.
    *King.* I have nothing with this answer, Hamlet. These
words are not mine.
    *Ham.* No, nor mine now. [*To Polonius*] My lord, you
played once i' the university, you say?     100
    *Pol.* That did I, my lord, and was accounted a good
actor.
    *Ham.* What did you enact?
    *Pol.* I did enact Julius Cæsar; I was killed i' the Capi-
tol; Brutus killed me.     105

Will Kemp performing his jig.
From the title page of Kemp's *Nine Daies Wonder* (1600).

108. **stay upon your patience:** await your willingness to hear them

116. **country:** indelicate, obscene

124. **your only jig-maker:** the best comic of them all

126. **'s:** this

129. **a suit of sables:** sable furs, then as now, were considered very rich attire; Hamlet also quibbles on the fact that black was called "sable" in heraldic terms.

132-33. **suffer not thinking on:** endure being forgotten; **the hobby-horse:** an imitation horse ridden in the May Day Morris dances. The reference here is to the suppression of hobby-horses by the Puritans, who regarded them as relics of heathenism.

*Ham.* It was a brute part of him to kill so capital a calf there. Be the players ready?

*Ros.* Ay, my lord. They stay upon your patience.

*Queen.* Come hither, my dear Hamlet, sit by me.

*Ham.* No, good mother, here's metal more attractive.   110

*Pol.* [*Aside to the King*] O, ho! do you mark that?

*Ham.* Lady, shall I lie in your lap?

*Oph.* No, my lord.

*Ham.* I mean, my head upon your lap?

*Oph.* Ay, my lord.   115

*Ham.* Do you think I meant country matters?

*Oph.* I think nothing, my lord.

*Ham.* That's a fair thought to lie between maids' legs.

*Oph.* What is, my lord?

*Ham.* Nothing.   120

*Oph.* You are merry, my lord.

*Ham.* Who, I?

*Oph.* Ay, my lord.

*Ham.* O God, your only jig-maker! What should a man do but be merry? For look you how cheerfully my mother 125 looks, and my father died within 's two hours.

*Oph.* Nay, 'tis twice two months, my lord.

*Ham.* So long? Nay then, let the devil wear black, for I'll have a suit of sables. O heavens! die two months ago, and not forgotten yet? Then there's hope a great man's 130 memory may outlive his life half a year. But, by'r Lady, he must build churches then; or else shall he suffer not thinking on, with the hobby-horse, whose epitaph is "For O, for O, the hobby-horse is forgot!"

Stage Dir. before 135. **Hautboys:** oboes

148. **miching malicho:** skulking crime. *Malhecho* is a Spanish word meaning "misdeed."

150. **Belike:** perhaps

158. **naught:** wicked (to speak so coarsely)

*Hautboys play. The dumb show enters.*

Enter a *King* and a *Queen* very lovingly; the *Queen* em-  13
bracing him. She kneels, and makes show of protestation
unto him. He takes her up, and declines his head upon
her neck. He lays him down upon a bank of flowers. She,
seeing him asleep, leaves him. Anon comes in a fellow,
takes off his crown, kisses it, pours poison in the *King's*  14
ears, and exits. The *Queen* returns, finds the *King* dead,
and makes passionate action. The *Poisoner*, with some two
or three *Mutes*, comes in again, seeming to lament with
her. The dead body is carried away. The *Poisoner* woos
the *Queen* with gifts; she seems loath and unwilling  14
awhile, but in the end accepts his love.

*Exeunt.*

*Oph.* What means this, my lord?

*Ham.* Marry, this is miching malicho; it means mis-
chief.

*Oph.* Belike this show imports the argument of the  15
play.

## Enter *Prologue*.

*Ham.* We shall know by this fellow. The players cannot keep counsel; they'll tell all.

*Oph.* Will he tell us what this show meant?

*Ham.* Ay, or any show that you'll show him. Be not  15
you ashamed to show, he'll not shame to tell you what it
means.

*Oph.* You are naught, you are naught! I'll mark the
play.

Neptune.
From Cartari, *Imagini delli Dei de gl'Antichi* (1674).

163. **posy:** motto
166. **Phœbus' cart:** the chariot of the sun god
167. **Neptune's salt wash:** the ocean; see I. i. 132;
**Tellus' orbed ground:** the earth, of which Tellus was the goddess among the Romans
170. **Hymen:** the Greek god of marriage
176. **distrust you:** fear for you
178. **holds quantity:** match in amount
179. **In neither aught, or in extremity:** that is, they either do not fear or love at all or they do so excessively.
185. **My operant powers their functions leave to do:** my faculties cease functioning.

*Pro.* For us, and for our tragedy,                          160
    *Here stooping to your clemency,*
    *We beg your hearing patiently.*          [Exit.]

*Ham.* Is this a prologue, or the posy of a ring?
*Oph.* 'Tis brief, my lord.
*Ham.* As woman's love.                                      165

    Enter [two *Players*,] *King* and *Queen*.

*King.* Full thirty times hath Phœbus' cart gone round
Neptune's salt wash and Tellus' orbed ground,
And thirty dozen moons with borrowed sheen
About the world have times twelve thirties been,
Since love our hearts, and Hymen did our hands,             170
Unite comutual in most sacred bands.
    *Queen.* So many journeys may the sun and moon
Make us again count o'er ere love be done!
But woe is me! you are so sick of late,
So far from cheer and from your former state,               175
That I distrust you. Yet, though I distrust,
Discomfort you, my lord, it nothing must;
For women's fear and love holds quantity,
In neither aught, or in extremity.
Now what my love is, proof hath made you know;              180
And as my love is sized, my fear is so.
Where love is great, the littlest doubts are fear;
Where little fears grow great, great love grows there.
    *King.* Faith, I must leave thee, love, and shortly too;
My operant powers their functions leave to do.              185
And thou shalt live in this fair world behind,
Honored, beloved, and haply one as kind
For husband shalt thou—

194. **instances:** inducements

195. **thrift:** financial advantage; see III. [ii.] 63.

200. **Purpose is but the slave to memory:** that is, a purpose must be remembered before it can be carried out.

201. **validity:** strength

204-5. **Most necessary 'tis that we forget/ To pay ourselves what to ourselves is debt:** our own resolution is but a promise made to ourselves and it is convenient to forget an obligation difficult to fulfill.

208-9. **The violence of either grief or joy/ Their own enactures with themselves destroy:** violent emotion wears itself out and destroys at the same time the impulses to action born with it.

211. **on slender accident:** because of trivial happenings

 *Queen.*     *O, confound the rest!*
*Such love must needs be treason in my breast.*  190
*In second husband let me be accurst!*
*None wed the second but who killed the first.*

 *Ham.* [*Aside*] Wormwood, wormwood!

 *Queen. The instances that second marriage move*
*Are base respects of thrift, but none of love.*  195
*A second time I kill my husband dead*
*When second husband kisses me in bed.*
 *King. I do believe you think what now you speak;*
*But what we do determine oft we break.*
*Purpose is but the slave to memory,*  200
*Of violent birth, but poor validity;*
*Which now, like fruit unripe, sticks on the tree,*
*But fall unshaken when they mellow be.*
*Most necessary 'tis that we forget*
*To pay ourselves what to ourselves is debt.*  205
*What to ourselves in passion we propose,*
*The passion ending, doth the purpose lose.*
*The violence of either grief or joy*
*Their own enactures with themselves destroy.*
*Where joy most revels, grief doth most lament;*  210
*Grief joys, joy grieves, on slender accident.*
*This world is not for aye, nor 'tis not strange*
*That even our loves should with our fortunes change;*
*For 'tis a question left us yet to prove,*
*Whether love lead fortune, or else fortune love.*  215
*The great man down, you mark his favorite flies,*
*The poor advanced makes friends of enemies;*

Hecate.
From Cartari, *Imagini delli Dei de gl'Antichi* (1674).
(See III. ii. 270.)

221. **seasons:** matures
231. **anchor's:** hermit's; **cheer:** fare
232. **opposite that blanks the face of joy:** contrary event that turns joy to sorrow
245. **argument:** summary of the plot

*And hitherto doth love on fortune tend,*
*For who not needs shall never lack a friend,*
*And who in want a hollow friend doth try,* 220
*Directly seasons him his enemy.*
*But, orderly to end where I begun,*
*Our wills and fates do so contrary run*
*That our devices still are overthrown;*
*Our thoughts are ours, their ends none of our own.* 225
*So think thou wilt no second husband wed;*
*But die thy thoughts when thy first lord is dead.*

*Queen.* Nor earth to me give food, nor heaven light,
*Sport and repose lock from me day and night,*
*To desperation turn my trust and hope,* 230
*An anchor's cheer in prison be my scope,*
*Each opposite that blanks the face of joy*
*Meet what I would have well, and it destroy,*
*Both here and hence pursue me lasting strife,*
*If, once a widow, ever I be wife!* 235

*Ham.* If she should break it now!

*King.* 'Tis deeply sworn. Sweet, leave me here awhile.
*My spirits grow dull, and fain I would beguile*
*The tedious day with sleep.*
    *Queen.*           *Sleep rock thy brain,* 240
                       *[He] sleeps.*
*And never come mischance between us twain!*    *Exit.*

*Ham.* Madam, how like you this play?
*Queen.* The lady doth protest too much, methinks.
*Ham.* O, but she'll keep her word.
*King.* Have you heard the argument? Is there no 245
offense in't?

250. **Tropically**: by a figure of speech. Hamlet conceives of the play as a trap for the King.

254. **free**: innocent; see II. ii. 570.

255. **Let the galled jade wince; our withers are unwrung**: what care we for the discomfort of the guilty; we are free in our own consciences.

257. **a chorus**: an actor who gave necessary background information on events not acted out in the play

259. **the puppets dallying**: Ophelia and her imagined lover making love. Puppet shows usually had a narrator interpreting the action.

262. **better, and worse**: more witty and more offensive

263. **So**: for better or worse, as stated in the marriage service

265. **the croaking raven doth bellow for revenge**: Hamlet parodies another contemporary play, *The True Tragedy of Richard III* (1594): "The screeking raven sits croaking for revenge."

268. **Confederate season, else no creature seeing**: the time suitable, with no spectators

269. **of midnight weeds collected**: collected from weeds at midnight and thus, according to popular belief about magic, more than ordinarily effective

270. **Hecate**: a Greek goddess, regarded in Shakespeare's time as the controller of magic and witchcraft; **ban**: curse

*Ham.* No, no! They do but jest, poison in jest; no offense i' the world.

*King.* What do you call the play?

*Ham.* "The Mousetrap." Marry, how? Tropically. This 250 play is the image of a murder done in Vienna. Gonzago is the duke's name: his wife, Baptista. You shall see anon. 'Tis a knavish piece of work; but what o' that? Your Majesty, and we that have free souls, it touches us not. Let the galled jade wince; our withers are unwrung. 255

### Enter *Lucianus.*

This is one Lucianus, nephew to the King.

*Oph.* You are as good as a chorus, my lord.

*Ham.* I could interpret between you and your love, if I could see the puppets dallying.

*Oph.* You are keen, my lord, you are keen. 260

*Ham.* It would cost you a groaning to take off my edge.

*Oph.* Still better, and worse.

*Ham.* So you must take your husbands.—Begin, murderer. Pox, leave thy damnable faces, and begin! Come, the croaking raven doth bellow for revenge. 265

*Luc. Thoughts black, hands apt, drugs fit, and time*
*   agreeing;*
*Confederate season, else no creature seeing;*
*Thou mixture rank, of midnight weeds collected,*
*With Hecate's ban thrice blasted, thrice infected,* 270
*Thy natural magic and dire property*
*On wholesome life usurp immediately.*

*Pours the poison in his ears.*

*Ham.* He poisons him i' the garden for's estate; his name's Gonzago. The story is extant, and writ in choice

278. **false fire:** a blank discharge, either of arms or fireworks

284. **ungalled:** uninjured

287-88. **a forest of feathers:** trimmings that an actor might wear; **if the rest of my fortunes turn Turk with me:** if my fortune so betrays me that I am reduced to such straits

288-89. **Provincial roses:** rosettes of ribbon. The damask rose was also known as *Rosa provincialis.*

289. **razed:** slashed in a decorative manner; **cry:** pack, usually applied to hunting dogs: "a cry of hounds"

293. **Damon:** applied to Horatio, whose loyal friendship Hamlet equates with that of Damon for Pythias

296. **pajock:** peacock, a creature of repulsive habits, according to contemporary natural history

Italian. You shall see anon how the murderer gets the 275
love of Gonzago's wife.

*Oph.* The King rises.

*Ham.* What, frighted with false fire?

*Queen.* How fares my lord?

*Pol.* Give o'er the play.                                    280

*King.* Give me some light! Away!

*All.* Lights, lights, lights!

            *Exeunt all but Hamlet and Horatio.*

*Ham.* Why, let the strucken deer go weep,
            The hart ungalled play;
        For some must watch, while some must sleep:    285
            Thus runs the world away.
Would not this, sir, and a forest of feathers—if the rest of
my fortunes turn Turk with me—with two Provincial
roses on my razed shoes, get me a fellowship in a cry of
players, sir?                                                290

*Hor.* Half a share.

*Ham.* A whole one I!
        For thou dost know, O Damon dear,
            This realm dismantled was
        Of Jove himself; and now reigns here        295
            A very, very—pajock.

*Hor.* You might have rhymed.

*Ham.* O good Horatio, I'll take the ghost's word for a
thousand pound! Didst perceive?

*Hor.* Very well, my lord.                                300

*Ham.* Upon the talk of the poisoning?

*Hor.* I did very well note him.

305. **perdy**: from French *par dieu*

311. **distempered**: disordered

313, 316. **choler**: anger, bile. Hamlet puns on the two meanings.

316. **purgation**: medicinal cleansing and spiritual purification are both meant.

324. **wholesome**: sane

The recorder demonstrated.
From John Hudgebut, *Thesaurus musicus* (1695).

*Ham.* Aha! Come, some music! Come, the recorders!
    For if the King like not the comedy,
      Why then, belike he likes it not, perdy.     305
Come, some music!

Enter *Rosencrantz* and *Guildenstern.*

*Guil.* Good my lord, vouchsafe me a word with you.

*Ham.* Sir, a whole history.

*Guil.* The King, sir—

*Ham.* Ay, sir, what of him?     310

*Guil.* Is in his retirement, marvellous distempered.

*Ham.* With drink, sir?

*Guil.* No, my lord; rather with choler.

*Ham.* Your wisdom should show itself more richer to signify this to his doctor; for, for me to put him to his 315 purgation would perhaps plunge him into far more choler.

*Guil.* Good my lord, put your discourse into some frame, and start not so wildly from my affair.

*Ham.* I am tame, sir; pronounce.

*Guil.* The Queen, your mother, in most great affliction 320 of spirit hath sent me to you.

*Ham.* You are welcome.

*Guil.* Nay, good my lord, this courtesy is not of the right breed. If it shall please you to make me a wholesome answer, I will do your mother's commandment; if not, 325 your pardon and my return shall be the end of my business.

*Ham.* Sir, I cannot.

*Guil.* What, my lord?

*Ham.* Make you a wholesome answer; my wit's dis- 330 eased. But, sir, such answer as I can make, you shall com-

334-35. **struck her into amazement and admiration**: paralyzed her with astonishment. **Amazement and admiration,** as used here, are practically synonymous.

344. **these pickers and stealers**: these hands. The Anglican Catechism forbids "picking and stealing."

348. **I lack advancement**: Hamlet attributes to himself a motive which he thinks Rosencrantz and Guildenstern will readily believe.

351. **"while the grass grows"**: the whole saying is "While the grass grows, the horse starves," which appears in literature as early as 1243.

354-55. **go about to recover the wind of me, as if you would drive me into a toil**: attempt to get on my windward side, where I cannot smell you out, in order to force me into a trap. Hamlet speaks as though they were hunters and he their quarry.

356-57. **if my duty be too bold, my love is too unmannerly**: if I offend you in following my duty, it is because my love conquers my manners.

359. **this pipe**: a recorder

mand; or rather, as you say, my mother. Therefore no
more, but to the matter! My mother, you say—

*Ros.* Then thus she says: your behavior hath struck
her into amazement and admiration.                    335

*Ham.* O wonderful son, that can so astonish a mother!
But is there no sequel at the heels of this mother's admiration? Impart.

*Ros.* She desires to speak with you in her closet ere
you go to bed.                                        340

*Ham.* We shall obey, were she ten times our mother.
Have you any further trade with us?

*Ros.* My lord, you once did love me.

*Ham.* And do still, by these pickers and stealers!

*Ros.* Good my lord, what is your cause of distemper? 345
You do surely bar the door upon your own liberty, if you
deny your griefs to your friend.

*Ham.* Sir, I lack advancement.

*Ros.* How can that be, when you have the voice of the
King himself for your succession in Denmark?          350

*Ham.* Ay, sir, but "while the grass grows"—the proverb
is something musty.

Enter the *Players* with recorders.

O, the recorders! Let me see one. To withdraw with you
—why do you go about to recover the wind of me, as if
you would drive me into a toil?                       355

*Guil.* O my lord, if my duty be too bold, my love is too
unmannerly.

*Ham.* I do not well understand that. Will you play
upon this pipe?

365. **ventages:** openings

368. **stops:** ventages

376. **organ:** a word applied to any musical instrument, especially a wind instrument

379. **fret:** besides the common meaning of **fret**, the word applies to the raised parts of stringed instruments by which the fingering is guided.

382. **presently:** at once; see II. ii. 599.

*Guil.* My lord, I cannot. 360
*Ham.* I pray you.
*Guil.* Believe me, I cannot.
*Ham.* I do beseech you.
*Guil.* I know no touch of it, my lord.
*Ham.* It is as easy as lying. Govern these ventages 365
with your finger and thumb, give it breath with your
mouth, and it will discourse most eloquent music. Look
you, these are the stops.
*Guil.* But these cannot I command to any utt'rance of
harmony. I have not the skill. 370
*Ham.* Why, look you now, how unworthy a thing you
make of me! You would play upon me; you would seem
to know my stops; you would pluck out the heart of my
mystery; you would sound me from my lowest note to
the top of my compass; and there is much music, excel- 375
lent voice, in this little organ, yet cannot you make it
speak. 'Sblood, do you think I am easier to be played on
than a pipe? Call me what instrument you will, though
you can fret me, you cannot play upon me.

Enter *Polonius.*

God bless you, sir! 380
*Pol.* My lord, the Queen would speak with you, and
presently.
*Ham.* Do you see yonder cloud that's almost in shape
of a camel?
*Pol.* By the mass, and 'tis like a camel indeed. 385
*Ham.* Methinks it is like a weasel.
*Pol.* It is backed like a weasel.

390. **by-and-by:** immediately

391. **They fool me to the top of my bent:** they force me to play the fool to the limit of my capacity. See the previous use of **bent** at II. ii. 32.

401. **Nero:** the Roman emperor who murdered his mother, Agrippina

405. **shent:** shamed

406. **give them seals:** authorize punitive action

||||||||||||||||||||||||||||||||||||||||||||||||||||

**III. [iii.]** Claudius instructs Rosencrantz and Guildenstern to accompany Hamlet to England. Polonius reports that Hamlet is on his way to Gertrude's room and hurries there to eavesdrop. Left alone, Claudius tries to pray. Hamlet, passing by, notices the opportunity for a deathblow, but rejects it with the excuse that he would send Claudius to heaven by killing him at such a moment of repentance.

||||||||||||||||||||||||||||||||||||||

3. **dispatch:** have drawn up

*Ham.* Or like a whale.

*Pol.* Very like a whale.

*Ham.* Then will I come to my mother by-and-by.— 390
They fool me to the top of my bent.—I will come by-and-
by.

*Pol.* I will say so.                                    *Exit.*

*Ham.* "By-and-by" is easily said.—Leave me, friends.
                              [*Exeunt all but Hamlet.*]
'Tis now the very witching time of night,                395
When churchyards yawn, and hell itself breathes out
Contagion to this world. Now could I drink hot blood
And do such bitter business as the day
Would quake to look on. Soft! now to my mother!
O heart, lose not thy nature; let not ever              400
The soul of Nero enter this firm bosom.
Let me be cruel, not unnatural;
I will speak daggers to her, but use none.
My tongue and soul in this be hypocrites—
How in my words somever she be shent,                   405
To give them seals never, my soul, consent!

                                               *Exit.*

[Scene III. The same. A room in the Castle.]

Enter *King, Rosencrantz,* and *Guildenstern.*

*King.* I like him not, nor stands it safe with us
To let his madness range. Therefore prepare you;
I your commission will forthwith dispatch,

5. **The terms of our estate**: my position as King

12. **peculiar**: personal, private

14. **noyance**: harm

15. **weal**: well-being

16. **cease**: termination

17. **gulf**: whirlpool

25. **Arm you . . . to**: prepare yourself for

31. **tax him home**: rebuke him effectively and completely

And he to England shall along with you.
The terms of our estate may not endure          5
Hazard so near us as doth hourly grow
Out of his lunacies.
  *Guil.*            We will ourselves provide.
Most holy and religious fear it is
To keep those many many bodies safe          10
That live and feed upon your Majesty.
  *Ros.* The single and peculiar life is bound
With all the strength and armor of the mind
To keep itself from noyance; but much more
That spirit upon whose weal depends and rests          15
The lives of many. The cease of majesty
Dies not alone, but like a gulf doth draw
What's near it with it. It is a massy wheel,
Fixed on the summit of the highest mount,
To whose huge spokes ten thousand lesser things          20
Are mortised and adjoined; which when it falls,
Each small annexment, petty consequence,
Attends the boist'rous ruin. Never alone
Did the king sigh, but with a general groan.
  *King.* Arm you, I pray you, to this speedy voyage;          25
For we will fetters put upon this fear,
Which now goes too free-footed.
  *Both.*            We will haste us.
                    *Exeunt Gentlemen.*


Enter *Polonius.*


  *Pol.* My lord, he's going to his mother's closet.
Behind the arras I'll convey myself          30
To hear the process. I'll warrant she'll tax him home;

33. **meet:** suitable

35. **of vantage:** from a favorable spot

40. **primal eldest curse:** the curse put upon Cain for murdering Abel

49-50. **Whereto serves mercy/ But to confront the visage of offense:** what purpose does mercy serve except to defend the sinner in the face of his sins.

59. **the offense:** his sinful profits, as enumerated in the preceding line

60. **corrupted currents:** wicked ways

61. **Offense's gilded hand:** the hand of a criminal improved with gold; **shove by:** elbow aside

And, as you said, and wisely was it said,
'Tis meet that some more audience than a mother,
Since nature makes them partial, should o'erhear
The speech, of vantage. Fare you well, my liege.                    35
I'll call upon you ere you go to bed
And tell you what I know.

    *King.*               Thanks, dear my lord.

                         *Exit [Polonius].*

O, my offense is rank, it smells to heaven;
It hath the primal eldest curse upon't,                             40
A brother's murder! Pray can I not,
Though inclination be as sharp as will.
My stronger guilt defeats my strong intent,
And, like a man to double business bound,
I stand in pause where I shall first begin,                         45
And both neglect. What if this cursed hand
Were thicker than itself with brother's blood,
Is there not rain enough in the sweet heavens
To wash it white as snow? Whereto serves mercy
But to confront the visage of offense?                              50
And what's in prayer but this twofold force,
To be forestalled ere we come to fall,
Or pardoned being down? Then I'll look up;
My fault is past. But, O, what form of prayer
Can serve my turn? "Forgive me my foul murder"?                     55
That cannot be; since I am still possessed
Of those effects for which I did the murder—
My crown, mine own ambition, and my queen.
May one be pardoned and retain the offense?
In the corrupted currents of this world                             60
Offense's gilded hand may shove by justice,

64-5. **There:** that is, in heaven; **the action lies/ In his true nature:** the action (in a legal sense) is admissible only on the basis of the true facts.

71. **limed:** trapped, like a bird caught in the sticky substance called birdlime

72. **engaged:** entangled

76. **pat:** opportunely

78. **That would be scanned:** that needs careful examination.

83. **grossly, full of bread:** in a gross condition, unfit for divine judgment because savoring of earthly pleasures and unconfessed

85. **audit:** the summing up of his life for judgment

And oft 'tis seen the wicked prize itself
Buys out the law; but 'tis not so above.
There is no shuffling; there the action lies
In his true nature, and we ourselves compelled,                65
Even to the teeth and forehead of our faults,
To give in evidence. What then? What rests?
Try what repentance can. What can it not?
Yet what can it when one cannot repent?
O wretched state! O bosom black as death!                70
O limed soul, that, struggling to be free,
Art more engaged! Help, angels! Make assay.
Bow, stubborn knees; and heart with strings of steel,
Be soft as sinews of the new-born babe!
All may be well.                          [*He kneels.*]   75

Enter *Hamlet.*

*Ham.* Now might I do it pat, now he is praying;
And now I'll do't. And so he goes to heaven,
And so am I revenged. That would be scanned.
A villain kills my father; and for that,
I, his sole son, do this same villain send          80
To heaven.
Why, this is hire and salary, not revenge!
He took my father grossly, full of bread,
With all his crimes broad blown, as flush as May;
And how his audit stands, who knows save heaven?   85
But in our circumstance and course of thought,
'Tis heavy with him; and am I then revenged,
To take him in the purging of his soul,
When he is fit and seasoned for his passage?
No.                                  90

91. **know thou a more horrid hent**: take advantage of a more terrible opportunity.

98. **stays**: awaits; see I. iii. 61.

99. **This physic but prolongs thy sickly days**: addressed to Claudius: this prayer merely prolongs your sinful days on earth, it does not cure your ills.

⎯⎯⎯⎯⎯⎯⎯⎯⎯⎯⎯⎯⎯⎯⎯⎯⎯⎯⎯

**III. [iv.]** Hamlet faces Gertrude in her chamber. His manner is so wild that she fears for her safety. Her outcry alarms Polonius, who calls for help. Hamlet stabs through the arras and kills him. Turning again to his mother, he rails at her for her sins, which he believes include complicity in his father's murder. The ghost enters to remind him of the revenge that he still must seek. Hamlet's discourse with the ghost, invisible to Gertrude, prompts her pity for what she takes to be a new proof of his lunacy. Hamlet asserts that his words are not mere madness and then leaves, dragging out Polonius' body. Hamlet's parting words reveal his suspicion of the King's treacherous motive in sending him to England and his resolve to turn the tables on Rosencrantz and Guildenstern.

⎯⎯⎯⎯⎯⎯⎯⎯⎯⎯⎯⎯⎯

2. **his pranks have been too broad**: he has taken too many liberties.

4. **I'll silence me even here**: I'll say no more than this.

5. **round**: outspoken; see II. ii. 149.

Up, sword, and know thou a more horrid hent.
When he is drunk asleep; or in his rage;
Or in the incestuous pleasure of his bed;
At gaming, swearing, or about some act
That has no relish of salvation in't—                           95
Then trip him, that his heels may kick at heaven,
And that his soul may be as damned and black
As hell, whereto it goes.  My mother stays.
This physic but prolongs thy sickly days.          *Exit.*
    *King.* [*Rises*] My words fly up, my thoughts remain 100
       below;
Words without thoughts never to heaven go.
                                                   *Exit.*

[Scene IV. The same. The *Queen's* closet.]

Enter *Queen* and *Polonius.*

    *Pol.* He will come straight. Look you lay home to him.
Tell him his pranks have been too broad to bear with,
And that your Grace hath screened and stood between
Much heat and him. I'll silence me even here.
Pray you be round with him.                              5
    *Ham.* [*Within*] Mother, mother, mother!
    *Queen.* I'll warrant you; fear me not. Withdraw; I
hear him coming.
                *[Polonius hides behind the arras.]*

12. **idle:** foolish
16. **forgot me:** forgotten who I am
17. **rood:** cross
28. **for a ducat:** I'll wager a ducat (a gold coin, worth several dollars).

Enter *Hamlet.*

*Ham.* Now, mother, what's the matter?

*Queen.* Hamlet, thou hast thy father much offended.     10

*Ham.* Mother, you have my father much offended.

*Queen.* Come, come, you answer with an idle tongue.

*Ham.* Go, go, you question with a wicked tongue.

*Queen.* Why, how now, Hamlet?

*Ham.*                              What's the matter now?     15

*Queen.* Have you forgot me?

*Ham.*                              No, by the rood, not so!

You are the Queen, your husband's brother's wife,

And—would it were not so—you are my mother.

*Queen.* Nay, then I'll set those to you that can speak.     20

*Ham.* Come, come, and sit you down, you shall not
    budge!

You go not till I set you up a glass

Where you may see the inmost part of you.

*Queen.* What wilt thou do? Thou wilt not murder me?     25

Help, help, ho!

*Pol.* [*Behind*] What, ho! help, help, help!

*Ham.* [*Draws*] How now? a rat? Dead for a ducat,
    dead!

        [*Stabs through the arras and*] *kills Polonius.*

*Pol.* [*Behind*] O, I am slain!     30

*Queen.*                              O me, what hast thou done?

*Ham.* Nay, I know not. Is it the King?

*Queen.* O, what a rash and bloody deed is this!

*Ham.* A bloody deed—almost as bad, good mother,

As kill a king, and marry with his brother.     35

44. **custom**: habit; **brazed**: hardened

45. **proof**: armor; **sense**: feeling

53. **a blister**: the result of a brand, such as whores received on the forehead

55. **contraction**: the marriage contract

56-7. **sweet religion makes/ A rhapsody of words**: makes the sanctified vows of marriage mere fanciful language

58. **this solidity and compound mass**: the globe of the earth

59. **tristful**: sad; **against the doom**: when Judgment Day looms. The meaning of the foregoing passage is that the whole world is sick at the thought of Gertrude's deed.

62. **That roars so loud and thunders in the index**: that receives such a violent introduction. **Index** means prefatory table of contents.

*Queen.* As kill a king?
*Ham.*                    Ay, lady, 'twas my word.
                    [*Pulls aside arras and sees Polonius.*]
Thou wretched, rash, intruding fool, farewell!
I took thee for thy better. Take thy fortune.
Thou find'st to be too busy is some danger.—                    40
Leave wringing of your hands. Peace! sit you down
And let me wring your heart; for so I shall
If it be made of penetrable stuff;
If damned custom have not brazed it so
That it is proof and bulwark against sense.                    45
    *Queen.* What have I done that thou dar'st wag thy
        tongue
In noise so rude against me?
    *Ham.*                    Such an act
That blurs the grace and blush of modesty;                    50
Calls virtue hypocrite; takes off the rose
From the fair forehead of an innocent love,
And sets a blister there; makes marriage vows
As false as dicers' oaths. O, such a deed
As from the body of contraction plucks                    55
The very soul, and sweet religion makes
A rhapsody of words! Heaven's face doth glow;
Yea, this solidity and compound mass,
With tristful visage, as against the doom,
Is thought-sick at the act.                    60
    *Queen.*                    Ay me, what act,
That roars so loud and thunders in the index?
    *Ham.* Look here upon this picture, and on this,
The counterfeit presentment of two brothers.
See what a grace was seated on this brow;                    65

66. **Hyperion:** a model of male beauty; see I. ii. 146; **front:** forehead

68. **station:** standing posture; **the herald Mercury:** the messenger of the Roman gods, also identified with the Greek Hermes

76. **leave to feed:** stop feeding

77. **batten:** gorge; **moor:** poor, waste land

80. **waits upon:** is subordinate to

81. **Sense:** sensual perception

87. **cozened:** cheated; **hoodman-blind:** blindman's buff

89. **sans:** without

92. **Rebellious hell:** Hamlet is apostrophizing the evil impulses in human nature which rebel against the virtuous.

96. **gives the charge:** attacks

Various aspects of Mercury.
From Cartari, *Imagini delli Dei de gl'Antichi* (1674).     89

Hyperion's curls; the front of Jove himself;
An eye like Mars, to threaten and command;
A station like the herald Mercury
New lighted on a heaven-kissing hill:
A combination and a form indeed                    70
Where every god did seem to set his seal
To give the world assurance of a man.
This was your husband. Look you now what follows.
Here is your husband, like a mildewed ear
Blasting his wholesome brother. Have you eyes?     75
Could you on this fair mountain leave to feed,
And batten on this moor? Ha! have you eyes?
You cannot call it love; for at your age
The heyday in the blood is tame, it's humble,
And waits upon the judgment; and what judgment     80
Would step from this to this? Sense sure you have,
Else could you not have motion; but sure that sense
Is apoplexed; for madness would not err,
Nor sense to ecstasy was ne'er so thralled
But it reserved some quantity of choice            85
To serve in such a difference. What devil was't
That thus hath cozened you at hoodman-blind?
Eyes without feeling, feeling without sight,
Ears without hands or eyes, smelling sans all,
Or but a sickly part of one true sense             90
Could not so mope.
O shame! where is thy blush? Rebellious hell,
If thou canst mutiny in a matron's bones,
To flaming youth let virtue be as wax
And melt in her own fire. Proclaim no shame        95
When the compulsive ardor gives the charge,

98. **reason panders will:** reason acts as a pander to desire instead of curbing it.

101. **grained:** fast dyed; "grain" was a permanent red dye.

102. **tinct:** color

104. **enseamed:** grease-laden

112. **a vice of kings:** a clown among kings. The Vice in morality plays was a comic role.

113. **cutpurse:** pickpocket

122. **lapsed in time and passion:** having wasted opportunity and failed to act on passionate impulse

Since frost itself as actively doth burn,
And reason panders will.
   *Queen.*         O Hamlet, speak no more!
Thou turn'st mine eyes into my very soul,          100
And there I see such black and grained spots
As will not leave their tinct.
   *Ham.*         Nay, but to live
In the rank sweat of an enseamed bed,
Stewed in corruption, honeying and making love    105
Over the nasty sty!
   *Queen.*      O, speak to me no more!
These words like daggers enter in mine ears.
No more, sweet Hamlet!
   *Ham.*         A murderer and a villain!     110
A slave that is not twentieth part the tithe
Of your precedent lord; a vice of kings;
A cutpurse of the empire and the rule,
That from a shelf the precious diadem stole
And put it in his pocket!              115
   *Queen.*         No more!

Enter *Ghost.*

   *Ham.* A king of shreds and patches!—
Save me and hover o'er me with your wings,
You heavenly guards! What would your gracious figure?
   *Queen.* Alas, he's mad!           120
   *Ham.* Do you not come your tardy son to chide,
That, lapsed in time and passion, lets go by
The important acting of your dread command?
O, say!

129. **Conceit:** imagination

134. **incorporal:** bodiless

143. **capable:** susceptible to emotional appeal; see III. [ii.] 11.

145. **effects:** deeds

146. **want:** lack; see I. ii. 156; **tears perchance for blood:** tears, perhaps, instead of bloody action

155. **habit:** dress

*Ghost.* Do not forget. This visitation          125
Is but to whet thy almost blunted purpose.
But look, amazement on thy mother sits.
O, step between her and her fighting soul!
Conceit in weakest bodies strongest works.
Speak to her, Hamlet.          130
  *Ham.*                How is it with you, lady?
  *Queen.* Alas, how is't with you,
That you do bend your eye on vacancy,
And with the incorporal air do hold discourse?
Forth at your eyes your spirits wildly peep;          135
And, as the sleeping soldiers in the alarm,
Your bedded hairs, like life in excrements,
Start up and stand on end. O gentle son,
Upon the heat and flame of thy distemper
Sprinkle cool patience! Whereon do you look?          140
  *Ham.* On him, on him! Look you how pale he glares!
His form and cause conjoined, preaching to stones,
Would make them capable.—Do not look upon me,
Lest with this piteous action you convert
My stern effects. Then what I have to do          145
Will want true color—tears perchance for blood.
  *Queen.* To whom do you speak this?
  *Ham.*                Do you see noth-
    ing there?
  *Queen.* Nothing at all; yet all that is I see.          150
  *Ham.* Nor did you nothing hear?
  *Queen.*                No, nothing but our-
    selves.
  *Ham.* Why, look you there! Look how it steals away!
My father, in his habit as he lived!          155
Look where he goes even now out at the portal!
                    *Exit Ghost.*

165. **gambol from:** leap away from erratically

166. **flattering unction:** soothing salve

171. **avoid what is to come:** refrain from the same sin in future.

174. **pursy:** fat and ill-conditioned; physically and morally slack

176. **curb:** bow

182-83. **That monster, custom, who all sense doth eat/ Of habits evil:** custom, which from common usage, destroys our awareness of evil habits. **Evil** is Theobald's correction of "devill" in the Second Quarto. The First Folio omits the passage.

184. **use:** habit

186. **aptly:** easily

*Queen.* This is the very coinage of your brain.
This bodiless creation ecstasy
Is very cunning in.

 *Ham.*   Ecstasy?        160
My pulse as yours doth temperately keep time
And makes as healthful music. It is not madness
That I have utt'red. Bring me to the test,
And I the matter will reword; which madness
Would gambol from. Mother, for love of grace,   165
Lay not that flattering unction to your soul,
That not your trespass but my madness speaks.
It will but skin and film the ulcerous place,
Whilst rank corruption, mining all within,
Infects unseen. Confess yourself to heaven;    170
Repent what's past; avoid what is to come;
And do not spread the compost on the weeds
To make them ranker. Forgive me this my virtue;
For in the fatness of these pursy times
Virtue itself of vice must pardon beg—     175
Yea, curb and woo for leave to do him good.

 *Queen.* O Hamlet, thou hast cleft my heart in twain.

 *Ham.* O, throw away the worser part of it,
And live the purer with the other half.
Good night—but go not to my uncle's bed.    180
Assume a virtue, if you have it not.
That monster, custom, who all sense doth eat
Of habits evil, is angel yet in this,
That to the use of actions fair and good
He likewise gives a frock or livery,     185
That aptly is put on. Refrain tonight,
And that shall lend a kind of easiness

190. **either . . . the devil:** the Second Quarto reads "either the devil"; the First Folio omits the whole passage. "And master" appears in the Fourth Quarto, from which many editors take the verb "master."

196. **their scourge and minister:** the instrument and agent of heaven's punishment

200. **remains behind:** is yet to come

206. **reechy:** reeking, foul smelling

212. **paddock:** toad; **gib:** tomcat

213. **Such dear concernings:** matters of such importance

215. **Unpeg:** unfasten

216. **the famous ape:** the story referred to is lost. Apparently the ape found a basket of birds on a roof top and let them out. Seeing them fly off, he got into the basket expecting to fly too, but fell to his death.

217. **try conclusions:** make an experiment

To the next abstinence; the next more easy;
For use almost can change the stamp of nature,
And either [. . .] the devil, or throw him out          190
With wondrous potency. Once more, good night;
And when you are desirous to be blest,
I'll blessing beg of you.—For this same lord,
I do repent; but heaven hath pleased it so,
To punish me with this, and this with me,          195
That I must be their scourge and minister.
I will bestow him, and will answer well
The death I gave him. So again, good night.
I must be cruel, only to be kind;
Thus bad begins, and worse remains behind.          200
One word more, good lady.
    *Queen.*                    What shall I do?
    *Ham.* Not this, by no means, that I bid you do:
Let the bloat King tempt you again to bed;
Pinch wanton on your cheek; call you his mouse;          205
And let him, for a pair of reechy kisses,
Or paddling in your neck with his damned fingers,
Make you to ravel all this matter out,
That I essentially am not in madness,
But mad in craft. 'Twere good you let him know;          210
For who that's but a queen, fair, sober, wise,
Would from a paddock, from a bat, a gib,
Such dear concernings hide? Who would do so?
No, in despite of sense and secrecy,
Unpeg the basket on the house's top,          215
Let the birds fly, and like the famous ape,
To try conclusions, in the basket creep
And break your own neck down.
    *Queen.* Be thou assured, if words be made of breath,

A petar.
From Guillet de Saint George, *Gentleman's dictionary* (1705).

229. **enginer:** engineer

230. **Hoist:** hoisted, blown skyward; **petar:** petard, a bomb

233. **two crafts directly meet:** the tactics of two enemies bring them into direct opposition.

234. **packing:** a pun: carrying off a burden (Polonius) and leaving the country

239. **to draw toward an end with you:** to come to the conclusion of my business

And breath of life, I have no life to breathe 220
What thou hast said to me.
  *Ham.* I must to England; you know that?
  *Queen.*                             Alack,
I had forgot! 'Tis so concluded on.
  *Ham.* There's letters sealed; and my two schoolfellows, 225
Whom I will trust as I will adders fanged,
They bear the mandate; they must swoop my way
And marshal me to knavery. Let it work;
For 'tis the sport to have the enginer
Hoist with his own petar; and 't shall go hard 230
But I will delve one yard below their mines
And blow them at the moon. O, 'tis most sweet
When in one line two crafts directly meet.
This man shall set me packing.
I'll lug the guts into the neighbor room.— 235
Mother, good night.—Indeed, this counsellor
Is now most still, most secret, and most grave,
Who was in life a foolish prating knave.
Come, sir, to draw toward an end with you.
Good night, mother. 240

                      *Exeunt (Hamlet lugging in*
                                    *Polonius).*

THE TRAGEDY OF

# HAMLET,

PRINCE OF DENMARK

ACT IV

**IV.** [i.] Gertrude reports Hamlet's impulsive killing of Polonius. Claudius sends Rosencrantz and Guildenstern to find Hamlet, and calls a meeting of the council of state.

▬▬▬▬▬▬▬▬▬▬▬▬▬▬

12. **brainish apprehension:** brainsick fancy

# ACT IV

[Scene I. Elsinore. A room in the Castle.]

*Enter King and Queen, with Rosencrantz and Guildenstern.*

*King.* There's matter in these sighs. These profound heaves
You must translate; 'tis fit we understand them.
Where is your son?
    *Queen.* Bestow this place on us a little while.      5
             *[Exeunt Rosencrantz and Guildenstern.]*
Ah, mine own lord, what have I seen tonight!
    *King.* What, Gertrude? How does Hamlet?
    *Queen.* Mad as the sea and wind when both contend
Which is the mightier. In his lawless fit,
Behind the arras hearing something stir,      10
Whips out his rapier, cries "A rat, a rat!"
And in this brainish apprehension kills
The unseen good old man.
    *King.*             O heavy deed!
It had been so with us, had we been there.      15
His liberty is full of threats to all—

95

19. **providence:** provision for the future

20. **short:** closely reined; **out of haunt:** away from other human contacts, solitary

27. **ore:** precious metal

34. **countenance:** sanction

42-3. **done. . . ./ Whose:** The Folio omits ll. 41-4 and the Second Quarto reads as here. The eighteenth-century editor Edward Capell suggested the insertion of the phrase, "So haply slander." A phrase of this general sense is required, and many editors follow Capell's suggestion.

44. **level:** well aimed; **his blank:** its target

To you yourself, to us, to every one.
Alas, how shall this bloody deed be answered?
It will be laid to us, whose providence
Should have kept short, restrained, and out of haunt        20
This mad young man. But so much was our love
We would not understand what was most fit,
But, like the owner of a foul disease,
To keep it from divulging, let it feed
Even on the pith of life. Where is he gone?        25
    *Queen.* To draw apart the body he hath killed,
O'er whom his very madness, like some ore
Among a mineral of metals base,
Shows itself pure. He weeps for what is done.
    *King.* O Gertrude, come away!        30
The sun no sooner shall the mountains touch
But we will ship him hence; and this vile deed
We must with all our majesty and skill
Both countenance and excuse. Ho, Guildenstern!

            Enter *Rosencrantz* and *Guildenstern*.

Friends both, go join you with some further aid.        35
Hamlet in madness hath Polonius slain,
And from his mother's closet hath he dragged him.
Go seek him out; speak fair, and bring the body
Into the chapel. I pray you haste in this.
            *Exeunt [Rosencrantz and Guildenstern].*
Come, Gertrude, we'll call up our wisest friends        40
And let them know both what we mean to do
And what's untimely done. [. . .]
Whose whisper o'er the world's diameter,
As level as the cannon to his blank,

46. **woundless:** invulnerable

||||||||||||||||||||||||||||||||||||||||||||||||||||||

**IV. [ii.]** Hamlet taunts Rosencrantz and Guildenstern when they question him about Polonius. He dashes away and forces them to pursue him.

||||||||||||||||||||||||||||||||||||||

12. **keep your counsel:** Hamlet promised to keep secret his knowledge that they were summoned.

13. **to be demanded of:** being questioned by; **replication:** reply

Transports his pois'ned shot—may miss our name          45
And hit the woundless air.—O, come away!
My soul is full of discord and dismay.

                                        *Exeunt.*

[Scene II. The same. A passage in the Castle.]


Enter *Hamlet.*

*Ham.* Safely stowed.
*Gentlemen.* (*Within*) Hamlet! Lord Hamlet!
*Ham.* But soft! What noise? Who calls on Hamlet? O,
here they come.


Enter *Rosencrantz* and *Guildenstern.*

*Ros.* What have you done, my lord, with the dead      5
    body?
*Ham.* Compounded it with dust, whereto 'tis kin.
*Ros.* Tell us where 'tis, that we may take it thence
And bear it to the chapel.
*Ham.* Do not believe it.                              10
*Ros.* Believe what?
*Ham.* That I can keep your counsel, and not mine own.
Besides, to be demanded of a sponge, what replication
should be made by the son of a king?
*Ros.* Take you me for a sponge, my lord?              15

16. **countenance:** patronage, favor

23-4. **a knavish speech sleeps in a foolish ear:** Hamlet implies that there is some question as to which of them is the knave and which the fool.

27-8. **The body is with the King, but the King is not with the body:** this is probably aimless talk to confuse the King; the meaning is not clear.

28, 30. **The King is a thing—/. . . Of nothing:** that is, the King is a mere mortal. Hamlet is both contemptuous and threatening.

30-1. **Hide fox, and all after:** the catch phrase for a game similar to hide-and-seek

⸻

**IV. [iii.]** Hamlet's slaying of Polonius is the pretext the King uses to command departure for England, to which Hamlet passively submits. Alone, the King indicates that his sealed orders call for Hamlet's death as soon as he arrives in England, because the King's safety demands it.

⸻

4. **distracted:** confused, of unstable judgment
6. **scourge:** punishment

*Ham.* Ay, sir, that soaks up the King's countenance,
his rewards, his authorities. But such officers do the King
best service in the end. He keeps them, like an ape, in the
corner of his jaw; first mouthed, to be last swallowed.
When he needs what you have gleaned, it is but squeez-    20
ing you and, sponge, you shall be dry again.

*Ros.* I understand you not, my lord.

*Ham.* I am glad of it: a knavish speech sleeps in a
foolish ear.

*Ros.* My lord, you must tell us where the body is and    25
go with us to the King.

*Ham.* The body is with the King, but the King is not
with the body. The King is a thing—

*Guil.* A thing, my lord?

*Ham.* Of nothing. Bring me to him. Hide fox, and all    30
after.

*Exeunt.*

_____

[Scene III. The same. A room as before.]


Enter *King.*


*King.* I have sent to seek him and to find the body.
How dangerous is it that this man goes loose!
Yet must not we put the strong law on him.
He's loved of the distracted multitude,
Who like not in their judgment, but their eyes;    5
And where 'tis so, the offender's scourge is weighed,

7. **bear all:** manage everything, carry it off

9. **Deliberate pause:** a carefully planned delay

23. **convocation of politic worms:** probably a reference to the famous Diet of Worms, summoned by the Emperor of the Holy Roman Empire in 1521 to hear the case of Martin Luther, with a sneer at Polonius' pretensions to statecraft

But never the offense. To bear all smooth and even,
This sudden sending him away must seem
Deliberate pause. Diseases desperate grown
By desperate appliance are relieved,       10
Or not at all.

*Enter Rosencrantz.*

         How now? What hath befall'n?
 *Ros.* Where the dead body is bestowed, my lord,
We cannot get from him.
   *King.*           But where is he?       15
   *Ros.* Without, my lord; guarded, to know your pleasure.
   *King.* Bring him before us.
   *Ros.* Ho, Guildenstern! Bring in my lord.

*Enter Hamlet and Guildenstern [with Attendants].*

   *King.* Now, Hamlet, where's Polonius?
   *Ham.* At supper.       20
   *King.* At supper? Where?
   *Ham.* Not where he eats, but where he is eaten. A certain convocation of politic worms are e'en at him. Your worm is your only emperor for diet. We fat all creatures else to fat us, and we fat ourselves for maggots. Your fat    25
king and your lean beggar is but variable service—two
dishes, but to one table. That's the end.
   *King.* Alas, alas!
   *Ham.* A man may fish with the worm that hath eat of a
king, and eat of the fish that hath fed of that worm.       30
   *King.* What dost thou mean by this?

33. **progress**: the term applied to the state journey of a monarch through his realm

42. **tender**: take care of; **dearly**: deeply, intensely; see I. ii. 191.

46. **tend**: await; **bent**: like a bow, ready to be released

52. **I see a cherub that sees them**: though Hamlet has not the omniscience of an angel, he has his suspicions of the King's purpose.

*Ham.* Nothing but to show you how a king may go a
progress through the guts of a beggar.

*King.* Where is Polonius?

*Ham.* In heaven. Send thither to see. If your messenger    35
find him not there, seek him i' the other place yourself.
But indeed, if you find him not within this month, you
shall nose him as you go up the stairs into the lobby.

*King.* Go seek him there. [*To Attendants.*]

*Ham.* He will stay till you come.                          40

[*Exeunt Attendants.*]

*King.* Hamlet, this deed, for thine especial safety,—
Which we do tender as we dearly grieve
For that which thou hast done,—must send thee hence
With fiery quickness. Therefore prepare thyself.
The bark is ready and the wind at help,                     45
The associates tend, and everything is bent
For England.

*Ham.*        For England?

*King.*                    Ay, Hamlet.

*Ham.*                              Good.                    50

*King.* So is it, if thou knew'st our purposes.

*Ham.* I see a cherub that sees them. But come, for
England! Farewell, dear mother.

*King.* Thy loving father, Hamlet.

*Ham.* My mother! Father and mother is man and wife;        55
man and wife is one flesh; and so, my mother. Come, for
England!                                                *Exit.*

*King.* Follow him at foot; tempt him with speed
   aboard;
Delay it not, I'll have him hence tonight.                  60
Away! for everything is sealed and done

63. **hold'st at aught:** value at all
64. **As my great power thereof may give thee sense:** as my great power may cause you to value my friendship
65. **cicatrice:** wound
66. **free:** freely given, without force
67. **coldly set:** value slightly
68. **process:** command
70. **present:** immediate
71. **the hectic:** a severe fever
73. **Howe'er my haps:** however my fortunes turn

**IV. [iv.]** Fortinbras and his army pass by Hamlet and his escorts. Hamlet compares the bravery and resolution of this son in his efforts to redress his father's losses with his own inactivity, and he again determines on bloody action.

3. **conveyance:** escort
5. **If that:** if
6. **in his eye:** before his person
9. **softly:** slowly

That else leans on the affair. Pray you make haste.
            [*Exeunt Rosencrantz and Guildenstern.*]
And, England, if my love thou hold'st at aught,—
As my great power thereof may give thee sense,
Since yet thy cicatrice looks raw and red                    65
After the Danish sword, and thy free awe
Pays homage to us,—thou mayst not coldly set
Our sovereign process, which imports at full,
By letters congruing to that effect,
The present death of Hamlet. Do it, England;                70
For like the hectic in my blood he rages,
And thou must cure me. Till I know 'tis done,
Howe'er my haps, my joys were ne'er begun.

                                            *Exit.*

[Scene IV. Near Elsinore Castle.]

Enter *Fortinbras* with his *Army* over the stage.

*For.* Go, Captain, from me greet the Danish king.
Tell him that by his license Fortinbras
Craves the conveyance of a promised march
Over his kingdom. You know the rendezvous.
If that his Majesty would aught with us,                    5
We shall express our duty in his eye;
And let him know so.
    *Capt.*            I will do't, my lord.
    *For.* Go softly on.
                        *Exeunt [all but the Captain].*

Military preparations.
From F. Vegetius, *De re militari* (1563).

18. **addition:** superfluous detail
21. **farm:** rent
23. **ranker:** greater; **in fee:** outright
27. **debate the question of this straw:** settle the argument, a mere straw, by battle
28. **imposthume:** internal festering growth
35. **dull:** sluggish
36. **market of his time:** commodity traded for his time

Enter *Hamlet, Rosencrantz,* [*Guildenstern,*] and others.

*Ham.* Good sir, whose powers are these?                    10
*Capt.* They are of Norway, sir.
*Ham.* How purposed, sir, I pray you?
*Capt.* Against some part of Poland.
*Ham.* Who commands them, sir?
*Capt.* The nephew to old Norway, Fortinbras.              15
*Ham.* Goes it against the main of Poland, sir,
Or for some frontier?
*Capt.* Truly to speak, and with no addition,
We go to gain a little patch of ground
That hath in it no profit but the name.                    20
To pay five ducats, five, I would not farm it;
Nor will it yield to Norway or the Pole
A ranker rate, should it be sold in fee.
*Ham.* Why, then the Polack never will defend it.
*Capt.* Yes, it is already garrisoned.                     25
*Ham.* Two thousand souls and twenty thousand ducats
Will not debate the question of this straw.
This is the imposthume of much wealth and peace,
That inward breaks, and shows no cause without
Why the man dies.—I humbly thank you, sir.                 30
*Capt.* God be wi' you, sir.                    [*Exit.*]
*Ros.*                    Will't please you go, my lord?
*Ham.* I'll be with you straight. Go a little before.
                    [*Exeunt all but Hamlet.*]
How all occasions do inform against me
And spur my dull revenge! What is a man,                   35
If his chief good and market of his time
Be but to sleep and feed? A beast, no more.

38. **discourse:** power of thought

39. **Looking before and after:** following an orderly process of reason from cause to effect

41. **fust:** mildew

47. **Sith:** since

48. **gross as earth:** as evident as the earth itself

55-8. **Rightly to be great/ Is not to stir without great argument,/ But greatly to find quarrel in a straw/ When honor's at the stake:** to be truly great is to require a powerful motive for action but to move on slight provocation when honor is involved.

63. **fantasy:** fancy; **trick of fame:** trifle to enhance the reputation

65. **Whereon the numbers cannot try the cause:** too small to hold the number of men involved

66. **continent:** receptacle

Defending honor in combat.
From Olaus Magnus, *Historia de gentibus septentrionalibus* (1555).

Sure he that made us with such large discourse,
Looking before and after, gave us not
That capability and godlike reason                          40
To fust in us unused. Now, whether it be
Bestial oblivion, or some craven scruple
Of thinking too precisely on the event,—
A thought which, quartered, hath but one part wisdom
And ever three parts coward,—I do not know                  45
Why yet I live to say "This thing's to do,"
Sith I have cause, and will, and strength, and means
To do't. Examples gross as earth exhort me.
Witness this army of such mass and charge,
Led by a delicate and tender prince,                        50
Whose spirit, with divine ambition puffed,
Makes mouths at the invisible event,
Exposing what is mortal and unsure
To all that fortune, death, and danger dare,
Even for an eggshell. Rightly to be great                   55
Is not to stir without great argument,
But greatly to find quarrel in a straw
When honor's at the stake. How stand I then,
That have a father killed, a mother stained,
Excitements of my reason and my blood,                      60
And let all sleep, while to my shame I see
The imminent death of twenty thousand men
That for a fantasy and trick of fame
Go to their graves like beds, fight for a plot
Whereon the numbers cannot try the cause,                   65
Which is not tomb enough and continent
To hide the slain? O, from this time forth,
My thoughts be bloody, or be nothing worth!

                                                *Exit.*

**IV. [v.]** The Queen hears of Ophelia's distracted behavior since her father's death and agrees to see her. All are shocked at her ravings. The King discloses that Laertes has had a report of Polonius' death and has returned to Denmark intent upon revenge. Laertes, with a rabble of supporters, forces his way into the presence of the King and Queen, but the King soon calms him and leads him away to talk in private about the circumstances of his father's death.

⁜⁜⁜⁜⁜⁜⁜⁜⁜⁜⁜⁜⁜⁜⁜⁜⁜⁜⁜⁜⁜⁜⁜⁜⁜

7. **Spurns enviously:** shies suspiciously

8-10. **Her speech is nothing,/ Yet the unshaped use of it doth move/ The hearers to collection:** she talks nonsense yet its formlessness moves her hearers to attempt to make a coherent narrative of what she says. Ophelia's mad talk is being interpreted in a way that may be dangerous to the King and Queen.

19. **(as sin's true nature is):** that is, sin is a disease of the soul.

20. **toy:** trifle; **amiss:** misfortune

21. **artless jealousy:** awkward suspicion

[Scene V. Elsinore. A room in the Castle.]

Enter *Queen, Horatio,* and a *Gentleman.*

*Queen.* I will not speak with her.
*Gent.* She is importunate, indeed distract;
Her mood will needs be pitied.
*Queen.*                              What would she have?
*Gent.* She speaks much of her father; says she hears    5
There's tricks i' the world, and hems, and beats her heart;
Spurns enviously at straws; speaks things in doubt,
That carry but half sense. Her speech is nothing,
Yet the unshaped use of it doth move
The hearers to collection; they aim at it,             10
And botch the words up fit to their own thoughts;
Which, as her winks and nods and gestures yield them,
Indeed would make one think there might be thought,
Though nothing sure, yet much unhappily.
*Hor.* 'Twere good she were spoken with; for she may  15
    strew
Dangerous conjectures in ill-breeding minds.
*Queen.* Let her come in.

                              [*Exit Gentleman.*]
[*Aside*] To my sick soul (as sin's true nature is)
Each toy seems prologue to some great amiss.            20
So full of artless jealousy is guilt
It spills itself in fearing to be spilt.

Enter *Ophelia* distracted.

*Oph.* Where is the beauteous Majesty of Denmark?
*Queen.* How now, Ophelia?

25-6. These lines resemble some in a popular song of the time beginning, "As you came from the holy land/ Of Walsingham," the author of which is unknown.

27. **cockle hat and staff:** parts of the garb of a pilgrim to the shrine of St. James of Compostela in Spain. A cockle shell was worn in the hatband of a returning pilgrim.

28. **shoon:** shoes

40. **Larded:** garnished

44-5. **God 'ild you:** God reward you; **the owl was a baker's daughter:** in an old story, the baker's daughter denied bread to Jesus and was changed to an owl.

47. **Conceit upon:** that is, she is too obsessed with him.

*Oph.* (Sings)
>    *How should I your true-love know*        25
>       *From another one?*
>    *By his cockle hat and staff*
>    *And his sandal shoon.*

*Queen.* Alas, sweet lady, what imports this song?
*Oph.* Say you? Nay, pray you mark.        30

(Sings) *He is dead and gone, lady,*
>       *He is dead and gone;*
>    *At his head a grass-green turf,*
>       *At his heels a stone.*

O, ho!        35
*Queen.* Nay, but Ophelia—
*Oph.* Pray you mark.

(Sings) *White his shroud as the mountain snow—*

Enter *King.*

*Queen.* Alas, look here, my lord!

*Oph.* (Sings)
>    *Larded all with sweet flowers;*        40
>    *Which bewept to the grave did not go*
>    *With true-love showers.*

*King.* How do you, pretty lady?
*Oph.* Well, God 'ild you! They say the owl was a
baker's daughter. Lord, we know what we are, but know        45
not what we may be. God be at your table!
*King.* Conceit upon her father.

51. **betime:** early
55. **dupped:** opened
60. **Gis:** an abbreviation for Jesus
63. **Cock:** a substitute for God

*Oph.* Pray let's have no words of this; but when they
ask you what it means, say you this:

(Sings) *Tomorrow is Saint Valentine's day,*                    50
    *All in the morning betime,*
*And I a maid at your window,*
    *To be your Valentine.*

    *Then up he rose and donned his clo'es*
        *And dupped the chamber door,*                    55
    *Let in the maid, that out a maid*
        *Never departed more.*

*King.* Pretty Ophelia!
*Oph.* Indeed, la, without an oath, I'll make an end on't!

[Sings] *By Gis and by Saint Charity,*                    60
    *Alack, and fie for shame!*
*Young men will do't if they come to't.*
    *By Cock, they are to blame.*

    *Quoth she, "Before you tumbled me,*
        *You promised me to wed."*                    65

He answers:
    *"So would I 'a' done, by yonder sun,*
        *An thou hadst not come to my bed."*

*King.* How long hath she been thus?
*Oph.* I hope all will be well. We must be patient; but I    70
cannot choose but weep to think they would lay him i' the
cold ground. My brother shall know of it; and so I thank
you for your good counsel. Come, my coach! Good night,
ladies. Good night, sweet ladies. Good night, good night.
                                                  *Exit.*

84. **greenly:** foolishly

85. **hugger-mugger:** secrecy

90. **Feeds on his wonder, keeps himself in clouds:** spends all his time speculating about his father's death and surrounds himself with the clouds of uncertainty

91. **buzzers:** gossips

93. **of matter beggared:** lacking any facts

95. **In ear and ear:** in every ear

96. **a murd'ring piece:** a cannon loaded with small missiles which scattered when it was fired

96-7. **in many places/ Gives me superfluous death:** wounds me in more places than are necessary to kill me

99. **Switzers:** Swiss guards, which many monarchs employed

103. **overpeering:** towering above; that is, overflowing; **list:** bound

*King.* Follow her close; give her good watch, I pray    75
  you.                                    [*Exit Horatio.*]
O, this is the poison of deep grief; it springs
All from her father's death. O Gertrude, Gertrude,
When sorrows come, they come not single spies,
But in battalions! First, her father slain;    80
Next, your son gone, and he most violent author
Of his own just remove; the people muddied,
Thick and unwholesome in their thoughts and whispers
For good Polonius' death, and we have done but greenly
In hugger-mugger to inter him; poor Ophelia    85
Divided from herself and her fair judgment,
Without the which we are pictures or mere beasts;
Last, and as much containing as all these,
Her brother is in secret come from France;
Feeds on his wonder, keeps himself in clouds,    90
And wants not buzzers to infect his ear
With pestilent speeches of his father's death,
Wherein necessity, of matter beggared,
Will nothing stick our person to arraign
In ear and ear. O my dear Gertrude, this,    95
Like to a murd'ring piece, in many places
Gives me superfluous death.            *A noise within.*
  *Queen.*                  Alack, what noise is this?
  *King.* Where are my Switzers? Let them guard the
    door.                                    100

### Enter a *Messenger.*

What is the matter?
  *Mess.*              Save yourself, my lord:
The ocean, overpeering of his list,
Eats not the flats with more impetuous haste

105. **in a riotous head**: heading a riotous force

109. **ratifiers and props of every word**: referring to **antiquity** and **custom**, which are the normal **ratifiers and props** of sound mottoes; **word**: motto; see I. [v.] 117.

114. **counter**: in the wrong direction, a term from hunting

126. **cuckold**: betrayed husband

131. **fear**: fear for

Than young Laertes, in a riotous head,                    105
O'erbears your officers. The rabble call him lord;
And, as the world were now but to begin,
Antiquity forgot, custom not known,
The ratifiers and props of every word,
They cry "Choose we, Laertes shall be king!"              110
Caps, hands, and tongues applaud it to the clouds,
"Laertes shall be king! Laertes king!"
                              *A noise within.*
 *Queen.* How cheerfully on the false trail they cry!
O, this is counter, you false Danish dogs!
 *King.* The doors are broke.                        115

    Enter *Laertes* with others.

 *Laer.* Where is this king?—Sirs, stand you all without.
 *All.* No, let's come in!
 *Laer.*    I pray you give me leave.
 *All.* We will, we will!
 *Laer.* I thank you. Keep the door.                  120
      [*Exeunt his Followers.*]
  O thou vile king,
Give me my father!
 *Queen.*   Calmly, good Laertes.
 *Laer.* That drop of blood that's calm proclaims me
  bastard;                                        125
Cries cuckold to my father; brands the harlot
Even here between the chaste unsmirched brows
Of my true mother.
 *King.*   What is the cause, Laertes,
That thy rebellion looks so giantlike?                    130
Let him go, Gertrude. Do not fear our person.

The "kind life-rend'ring pelican."
From *An Early English Version of Hortus Sanitatis* (1954).

133. **peep:** that is, look at from a distance

147. **throughly:** thoroughly

148. **stay:** hinder

149. **My will, not all the world:** I shall have my will and nothing will stop me.

155. **swoopstake:** indiscriminately, as in a game of chance one might gather up all the winnings, regardless of who won or lost

160. **life-rend'ring pelican:** Elizabethan natural history reported that the pelican fed its young with her own flesh and blood by tearing her breast.

There's such divinity doth hedge a king
That treason can but peep to what it would,
Acts little of his will. Tell me, Laertes,
Why thou art thus incensed. Let him go, Gertrude.        135
Speak, man.

    *Laer.* Where is my father?

    *King.*                              Dead.

    *Queen.*                              But not by him!

    *King.* Let him demand his fill.        140

    *Laer.* How came he dead? I'll not be juggled with:
To hell, allegiance! vows, to the blackest devil!
Conscience and grace, to the profoundest pit!
I dare damnation. To this point I stand,
That both the worlds I give to negligence,        145
Let come what comes; only I'll be revenged
Most throughly for my father.

    *King.*                              Who shall stay you?

    *Laer.* My will, not all the world!
And for my means, I'll husband them so well        150
They shall go far with little.

    *King.*                              Good Laertes,
If you desire to know the certainty
Of your dear father's death, is't writ in your revenge
That swoopstake you will draw both friend and foe,        155
Winner and loser?

    *Laer.* None but his enemies.

    *King.*                              Will you know them then?

    *Laer.* To his good friends thus wide I'll ope my arms
And, like the kind life-rend'ring pelican,        160
Repast them with my blood.

    *King.*                              Why, now you speak
Like a good child and a true gentleman.

171. **virtue:** power

177. **Nature is fine in love:** human nature is noble in love.

186-87. **You must sing "A-down, a-down," and you, "Call him a-down-a":** both phrases are from the chorus of a song but to the hearer they may seem applicable to Polonius; **wheel:** spinning wheel. Ophelia is remembering songs she heard women sing as they worked at their spinning wheels.

188. **false steward:** probably a reference to a forgotten story

189. **This nothing's more than matter:** this nonsense is more eloquent than a full recital of her distress.

That I am guiltless of your father's death,
And am most sensibly in grief for it,                    165
It shall as level to your judgment pierce
As day does to your eye.

         *A noise within:* "Let her come in."

  *Laer.* How now? What noise is that?

         Enter *Ophelia.*

O heat, dry up my brains! Tears seven times salt          170
Burn out the sense and virtue of mine eye!
By heaven, thy madness shall be paid by weight
Till our scale turn the beam. O rose of May!
Dear maid, kind sister, sweet Ophelia!
O heavens! is't possible a young maid's wits              175
Should be as mortal as an old man's life?
Nature is fine in love, and where 'tis fine,
It sends some precious instance of itself
After the thing it loves.

  *Oph.* (*Sings*)

      *They bore him barefaced on the bier*          18(
        (*Hey non nony, nony, hey nony*)
      *And in his grave rained many a tear.*

Fare you well, my dove!

  *Laer.* Hadst thou thy wits, and didst persuade revenge,
It could not move thus.                                   18£

  *Oph.* You must sing "A-down, a-down," and you, "Call
him a-down-a." O, how the wheel becomes it! It is the
false steward, that stole his master's daughter.

  *Laer.* This nothing's more than matter.

  *Oph.* There's rosemary, that's for remembrance. Pray  19(

193. **document:** lesson

195-98. The plants mentioned have the following symbolism: **fennel,** flattery; **columbines,** disloyalty or ingratitude; **rue,** both sorrow and repentance; **daisies,** infidelity; **violets,** faithfulness. Ophelia in her madness goes through the motions of distributing flowers, the meaning of which would have been plain to an Elizabethan audience.

196-97. **herb of grace:** the plant associated with repentance might appropriately be called the herb of divine grace.

198. **a difference:** a heraldic term for a variation in a coat of arms to distinguish among different branches of a family. Presumably Ophelia has given rue to the King or the Queen; their grief has a different origin than hers, and their need for repentance will be obvious to the audience.

202. **passion:** grief

203. **favor:** attractiveness

210. **poll:** head, here referring to its thatch of hair

you, love, remember. And there is pansies, that's for
thoughts.

*Laer.* A document in madness! Thoughts and remembrance fitted.

*Oph.* There's fennel for you, and columbines. There's 195
rue for you, and here's some for me. We may call it herb
of grace o' Sundays. O, you must wear your rue with a
difference! There's a daisy. I would give you some violets,
but they withered all when my father died. They say he
made a good end.                                          200

[*Sings*] *For bonny sweet Robin is all my joy.*

*Laer.* Thought and affliction, passion, hell itself,
She turns to favor and to prettiness.

*Oph.* (*Sings*)

   *And will he not come again?*
   *And will he not come again?*              205
    *No, no, he is dead;*
    *Go to thy deathbed;*
   *He never will come again.*

   *His beard was as white as snow,*
   *All flaxen was his poll.*                     210
    *He is gone, he is gone,*
    *And we cast away moan.*
   *God 'a' mercy on his soul!*

And of all Christian souls, I pray God. God be wi' you.
           *Exit.*

*Laer.* Do you see this, O God?                            215
*King.* Laertes, I must commune with your grief,
Or you deny me right. Go but apart,
Make choice of whom your wisest friends you will,

220. **collateral**: indirect
229. **hatchment**: a tablet bearing his arms

||||||||||||||||||||||||||||||||||||||||||||||||||||||||||||||||||

**IV.** [**vi.**] Horatio receives a message from Hamlet reporting his capture by pirates and his return alone to Denmark. Horatio, as instructed, leaves with the bearers of the letter to find Hamlet.

And they shall hear and judge 'twixt you and me.
If by direct or by collateral hand
They find us touched, we will our kingdom give,   220
Our crown, our life, and all that we call ours,
To you in satisfaction; but if not,
Be you content to lend your patience to us,
And we shall jointly labor with your soul   225
To give it due content.
 *Laer.*    Let this be so.
His means of death, his obscure funeral—
No trophy, sword, nor hatchment o'er his bones,
No noble rite nor formal ostentation,—   230
Cry to be heard, as 'twere from heaven to earth,
That I must call't in question.
 *King.*    So you shall;
And where the offense is let the great axe fall.
I pray you go with me.   235

        *Exeunt.*

[Scene VI. The same. Another room in the Castle.]

Enter *Horatio* with an *Attendant.*

*Hor.* What are they that would speak with me?
*Servant.* Sailors, sir. They say they have letters for
 you.
*Hor.* Let them come in.

       [*Exit Attendant.*]
I do not know from what part of the world   5
I should be greeted, if not from Lord Hamlet.

Nauicularius Brit annus. quem Britonem vulgo nominat.

An Italian notion of an English sailor of the sixteenth century. From Bertelli, *Diversarum nationum habitum* (1594).

16. **appointment:** equipment

20-1. **thieves of mercy:** merciful thieves

25-6. **too light for the bore of the matter:** too light for the caliber of the gun; in other words, inadequate

30. **way:** admittance

Enter *Sailors*.

*Sailor.* God bless you, sir.

*Hor.* Let him bless thee too.

*Sailor.* He shall, sir, an't please him. There's a letter for you, sir,—it comes from the ambassador that was bound for England—if your name be Horatio, as I am let to know it is. 10

*Hor.* (*Reads the letter.*) *Horatio, when thou shalt have overlooked this, give these fellows some means to the King. They have letters for him. Ere we were two days old at sea, a pirate of very warlike appointment gave us chase. Finding ourselves too slow of sail, we put on a compelled valor, and in the grapple I boarded them. On the instant they got clear of our ship; so I alone became their prisoner. They have dealt with me like thieves of mercy; but they knew what they did: I am to do a good turn for them. Let the King have the letters I have sent, and repair thou to me with as much speed as thou wouldst fly death. I have words to speak in thine ear will make thee dumb; yet are they much too light for the bore of the matter. These good fellows will bring thee where I am. Rosencrantz and Guildenstern hold their course for England. Of them I have much to tell thee. Farewell.* 15 20 25

　　　　　*He that thou knowest thine,* HAMLET.

Come, I will give you way for these your letters, 30
And do't the speedier that you may direct me
To him from whom you brought them.

　　　　　　　　　　　　　*Exeunt.*

**IV. [vii.]** Claudius and Laertes are interrupted by the delivery of letters from Hamlet announcing his imminent return. Having failed to dispose of Hamlet, Claudius devises his certain death in a fencing match with Laertes. Laertes will poison his rapier, and in case that fails, Claudius will provide a poisoned drink. They have just agreed on this plan when Gertrude enters to report the drowning of Ophelia.

᠁᠁᠁᠁᠁᠁᠁᠁᠁᠁᠁᠁᠁᠁

10. **mainly:** mightily
16. **conjunctive:** joined with, inseparable from
19. **count:** reckoning
20. **general gender:** common people
22. **the spring that turneth wood to stone:** several English springs were known for petrifying wood, including one in Shakespeare's own county of Warwickshire.
23. **gyves:** shackles

[Scene VII. The same. Another room in the Castle.]

Enter *King* and *Laertes*.

*King.* Now must your conscience my acquittance seal,
And you must put me in your heart for friend,
Sith you have heard, and with a knowing ear,
That he which hath your noble father slain
Pursued my life.                                        5
*Laer.*          It well appears. But tell me
Why you proceeded not against these feats
So crimeful and so capital in nature,
As by your safety, wisdom, all things else,
You mainly were stirred up.                             10
*King.*                    O, for two special reasons,
Which may to you, perhaps, seem much unsinewed,
But yet to me they are strong. The Queen his mother
Lives almost by his looks; and for myself,—
My virtue or my plague, be it either which,—           15
She's so conjunctive to my life and soul
That, as the star moves not but in his sphere,
I could not but by her. The other motive
Why to a public count I might not go
Is the great love the general gender bear him,         20
Who, dipping all his faults in their affection,
Would, like the spring that turneth wood to stone,
Convert his gyves to graces; so that my arrows,
Too slightly timbered for so loud a wind,
Would have reverted to my bow again,                   25
And not where I had aimed them.

28. **terms:** conditions

29. **back again:** to the past before her reason failed

30. **Stood challenger on mount of all the age:** was unrivaled throughout the world

48. **naked:** defenseless

*Laer.* And so have I a noble father lost;
A sister driven into desp'rate terms,
Whose worth, if praises may go back again,
Stood challenger on mount of all the age          30
For her perfections. But my revenge will come.
    *King.* Break not your sleeps for that. You must not think
That we are made of stuff so flat and dull
That we can let our beard be shook with danger,
And think it pastime. You shortly shall hear more.          35
I loved your father, and we love ourself,
And that, I hope, will teach you to imagine—

Enter a *Messenger* with letters.

How now? What news?
    *Mess.*                    Letters, my lord, from Hamlet:
This to your Majesty; this to the Queen.          40
    *King.* From Hamlet? Who brought them?
    *Mess.* Sailors, my lord, they say; I saw them not.
They were given me by Claudio; he received them
Of him that brought them.
    *King.*                    Laertes, you shall hear them.          45
Leave us.

*Exit Messenger.*

    [*Reads*] *High and Mighty,—You shall know I am set
naked on your kingdom. Tomorrow shall I beg leave to
see your kingly eyes; when I shall (first asking your pardon thereunto) recount the occasion of my sudden and*          50
*more strange return.*                    HAMLET.

What should this mean? Are all the rest come back?
Or is it some abuse, and no such thing?

Posture of defense with rapier and dagger.
From George Silver, *Paradoxes of defence* (1599).

55. **character**: handwriting

69. **checking at**: shying from, a term from falconry

74. **uncharge the practice**: acquit the method of treachery

79. **falls right**: accords with my plan

82. **parts**: abilities

85. **siege**: seat, that is, rank

*Laer.* Know you the hand?

*King.*                    'Tis Hamlet's character.    55
  "Naked!"

And in a postscript here, he says "alone."

Can you advise me?

  *Laer.* I am lost in it, my lord. But let him come!

It warms the very sickness in my heart    60

That I shall live and tell him to his teeth,

"Thus didest thou."

  *King.*         If it be so, Laertes

(As how should it be so? how otherwise?),

Will you be ruled by me?    65

  *Laer.*            Ay, my lord,

So you will not o'errule me to a peace.

  *King.* To thine own peace. If he be now returned,

As checking at his voyage, and that he means

No more to undertake it, I will work him    70

To an exploit now ripe in my device,

Under the which he shall not choose but fall;

And for his death no wind of blame shall breathe,

But even his mother shall uncharge the practice

And call it accident.    75

  *Laer.*         My lord, I will be ruled;

The rather, if you could devise it so

That I might be the organ.

  *King.*            It falls right.

You have been talked of since your travel much,    80

And that in Hamlet's hearing, for a quality

Wherein they say you shine. Your sum of parts

Did not together pluck such envy from him

As did that one; and that, in my regard,

Of the unworthiest siege.    85

87. **A very riband in the cap of youth:** a mere decorative accessory to youth

89. **livery:** uniform, characteristic dress

90. **weeds:** garments

91. **health:** lack of concern about considerations of health. This applies to the **light and careless livery** of youth; **graveness:** sober dignity; **since:** ago

97. **incorpsed and demi-natured:** grown into the same body with (his horse) to form a centaur

98. **brave:** noble; **topped my thought:** surpassed what I could imagine

99. **in forgery of shapes and tricks:** in imagining feats of horsemanship

107. **made confession of you:** admitted knowing you

112. **scrimers:** fencers

*Laer.*                What part is that, my lord?
  *King.* A very riband in the cap of youth—
Yet needful too; for youth no less becomes
The light and careless livery that it wears
Than settled age his sables and his weeds,                    90
Importing health and graveness. Two months since
Here was a gentleman of Normandy.
I have seen myself, and served against, the French,
And they can well on horseback; but this gallant
Had witchcraft in't. He grew unto his seat,                    95
And to such wondrous doing brought his horse
As had he been incorpsed and demi-natured
With the brave beast. So far he topped my thought
That I, in forgery of shapes and tricks,
Come short of what he did.                                    100
  *Laer.*                A Norman was't?
  *King.* A Norman.
  *Laer.* Upon my life, Lamound.
  *King.*                The very same.
  *Laer.* I know him well. He is the brooch indeed            105
And gem of all the nation.
  *King.* He made confession of you;
And gave you such a masterly report
For art and exercise in your defense,
And for your rapier most especially,                          110
That he cried out 'twould be a sight indeed
If one could match you. The scrimers of their nation
He swore had neither motion, guard, nor eye,
If you opposed them. Sir, this report of his
Did Hamlet so envenom with his envy                           115
That he could nothing do but wish and beg

126. **in passages of proof:** by happenings which prove it

131. **plurisy:** excess

136-37. **a spendthrift sigh,/ That hurts by easing:** though the sigh eases distress, it is harmful to the constitution. Sighs were supposed to draw blood from the heart and weaken its action.

146. **put on:** incite

148. **in fine:** finally

Your sudden coming o'er to play with him.
Now, out of this—
  *Laer.*        What out of this, my lord?
  *King.* Laertes, was your father dear to you?        120
Or are you like the painting of a sorrow,
A face without a heart?
  *Laer.*        Why ask you this?
  *King.* Not that I think you did not love your father;
But that I know love is begun by time,        125
And that I see, in passages of proof,
Time qualifies the spark and fire of it.
There lives within the very flame of love
A kind of wick or snuff that will abate it;
And nothing is at a like goodness still;        130
For goodness, growing to a plurisy,
Dies in his own too-much. That we would do,
We should do when we would; for this "would" changes,
And hath abatements and delays as many
As there are tongues, are hands, are accidents;        135
And then this "should" is like a spendthrift sigh,
That hurts by easing. But to the quick o' the ulcer!
Hamlet comes back. What would you undertake
To show yourself your father's son in deed
More than in words?        140
  *Laer.*        To cut his throat i' the church!
  *King.* No place indeed should murder sanctuarize;
Revenge should have no bounds. But, good Laertes,
Will you do this? Keep close within your chamber.
Hamlet returned shall know you are come home.        145
We'll put on those shall praise your excellence
And set a double varnish on the fame
The Frenchman gave you; bring you in fine together

153. **unbated**: unblunted. A mere contest of skill would be fought with blunt rapiers, and Claudius counts on Hamlet's taking this for granted; **a pass of practice**: a treacherous thrust.

157. **mountebank**: quack

159. **cataplasm**: poultice

160. **simples**: herbs

167. **May fit us to our shape**: may suit our design

168. **drift**: intention

169. **'Twere**: it would be

171. **blast in proof**: fail in the trial

172. **your cunnings**: your respective skills

173. **ha't**: have it

177. **nonce**: specific purpose

178. **stuck**: thrust, a fencing term

179. **hold**: prevail

And wager on your heads.  He, being remiss,
Most generous, and free from all contriving,                150
Will not peruse the foils; so that with ease,
Or with a little shuffling, you may choose
A sword unbated, and, in a pass of practice,
Requite him for your father.
    *Laer.*             I will do't!                155
And for that purpose I'll anoint my sword.
I bought an unction of a mountebank,
So mortal that, but dip a knife in it,
Where it draws blood no cataplasm so rare,
Collected from all simples that have virtue                160
Under the moon, can save the thing from death
That is but scratched withal.  I'll touch my point
With this contagion, that, if I gall him slightly,
It may be death.
    *King.*       Let's further think of this,                165
Weigh what convenience both of time and means
May fit us to our shape.  If this should fail,
And that our drift look through our bad performance,
'Twere better not assayed.  Therefore this project
Should have a back or second, that might hold                170
If this did blast in proof.  Soft! let me see.
We'll make a solemn wager on your cunnings—
I ha't!
When in your motion you are hot and dry—
As make your bouts more violent to that end—                175
And that he calls for drink, I'll have prepared him
A chalice for the nonce; whereon but sipping,
If he by chance escape your venomed stuck,
Our purpose may hold there.—But stay, what noise?

187. **long purples:** a species of orchid
188. **liberal:** plain-spoken
191. **sliver:** branch
196. **incapable of:** insensible to
197. **indued:** adapted
206. **our trick:** the way of humans

Enter *Queen*.

How now, sweet queen?                                                    180
   *Queen.* One woe doth tread upon another's heel,
So fast they follow. Your sister's drowned, Laertes.
   *Laer.* Drowned! O, where?
   *Queen.* There is a willow grows aslant a brook,
That shows his hoar leaves in the glassy stream.                         185
There with fantastic garlands did she come
Of crowflowers, nettles, daisies, and long purples,
That liberal shepherds give a grosser name,
But our cold maids do dead men's fingers call them.
There on the pendent boughs her coronet weeds                           190
Clamb'ring to hang, an envious sliver broke,
When down her weedy trophies and herself
Fell in the weeping brook. Her clothes spread wide
And, mermaid-like, awhile they bore her up;
Which time she chanted snatches of old tunes,                           195
As one incapable of her own distress,
Or like a creature native and indued
Unto that element; but long it could not be
Till that her garments, heavy with their drink,
Pulled the poor wretch from her melodious lay                           200
To muddy death.
   *Laer.*        Alas, then she is drowned?
   *Queen.* Drowned, drowned.
   *Laer.* Too much of water hast thou, poor Ophelia,
And therefore I forbid my tears; but yet                                 205
It is our trick; nature her custom holds,
Let shame say what it will. When these are gone,

208. **The woman will be out**: my feminine weakness will be exhausted.

209. **fain would**: is eager to

210. **douts**: extinguishes; see I. [iv.] 40.

The woman will be out. Adieu, my lord.
I have a speech of fire, that fain would blaze
But that this folly douts it.                                    *Exit.* 210
   *King.*                 Let's follow, Gertrude.
How much I had to do to calm his rage!
Now fear I this will give it start again;
Therefore let's follow.

                                 *Exeunt.*

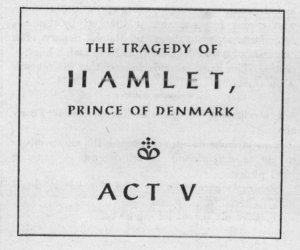

THE TRAGEDY OF

# HAMLET,

PRINCE OF DENMARK

# ACT V

**V. [i.]** Hamlet and Horatio come upon two rustics digging a grave. A funeral party, including the King and Queen and Laertes, enters, and Hamlet soon discovers that the corpse is that of Ophelia. Laertes' melodramatic expressions of grief incense Hamlet, who comes forward and is attacked by Laertes. Attendants separate them and Hamlet departs after expressing his own love for Ophelia to match Laertes' ranting. The King reminds Laertes that his revenge is imminent.

〰〰〰〰〰〰〰〰〰〰〰

4. **straight:** at once; see II. ii. 439; **crowner:** coroner

9. **se offendendo:** in self-offense; the clown means to say *se defendendo*, in self-defense, a common legal phrase.

12. **argal:** a mistake for *ergo*, the Latin "therefore," a term from formal logic

15. **Give me leave:** let me go on.

# ACT V

[Scene I. The same. A churchyard.]

*Enter two* Clowns, [with spades and pickaxes].

*Clown.* Is she to be buried in Christian burial that wilfully seeks her own salvation?

*Other.* I tell thee she is; therefore make her grave straight. The crowner hath sat on her, and finds it Christian burial.                                             5

*Clown.* How can that be, unless she drowned herself in her own defense?

*Other.* Why, 'tis found so.

*Clown.* It must be *se offendendo;* it cannot be else. For here lies the point: if I drown myself wittingly, it   10 argues an act; and an act hath three branches—it is to act, to do, and to perform; argal, she drowned herself wittingly.

*Other.* Nay, but hear you, Goodman Delver!

*Clown.* Give me leave. Here lies the water; good.   15 Here stands the man; good. If the man go to this water and drown himself, it is, will he nill he, he goes—mark you that. But if the water come to him and drown him, he drowns not himself. Argal, he that is not guilty of his own death shortens not his own life.                         20

*Other.* But is this law?

122

Adam with his spade.
From the Trevelyon MS. (c. 1608).

22. **quest:** inquest
26. **there thou say'st:** you said it.
27. **count'nance:** sanction; see IV. [i.] 34.
28. **their even-Christian:** their fellow Christian
30. **hold up:** maintain

33. **He was the first that ever bore arms:** the heraldic shield is shaped like a spade, and Adam's spade is shown in some books of heraldry as the oldest escutcheon. Only gentlemen had the right to possess coats of arms.

38-9. **confess thyself:** a common proverb: "Confess thyself and be hanged."

40. **Go to:** get along with you; see I. iii. 118.

*Clown.* Ay, marry, is't—crowner's quest law.

*Other.* Will you ha' the truth on't? If this had not been a gentlewoman, she should have been buried out o' Christian burial. 25

*Clown.* Why, there thou say'st! And the more pity that great folk should have count'nance in this world to drown or hang themselves more than their even-Christian. Come, my spade! There is no ancient gentlemen but gard'ners, ditchers, and grave-makers. They hold up Adam's profession. 30

*Other.* Was he a gentleman?

*Clown.* He was the first that ever bore arms.

*Other.* Why, he had none.

*Clown.* What, art a heathen? How dost thou understand the Scripture? The Scripture says Adam digged. Could he dig without arms? I'll put another question to thee. If thou answerest me not to the purpose, confess thyself— 35

*Other.* Go to! 40

*Clown.* What is he that builds stronger than either the mason, the shipwright, or the carpenter?

*Other.* The gallows-maker; for that frame outlives a thousand tenants.

*Clown.* I like thy wit well, in good faith. The gallows does well. But how does it well? It does well to those that do ill. Now, thou dost ill to say the gallows is built stronger than the church. Argal, the gallows may do well to thee. To't again, come! 45

*Other.* Who builds stronger than a mason, a shipwright, or a carpenter? 50

52. **unyoke:** unharness, your day's work is done.

55. **Mass:** by the Mass

60. **Yaughan:** presumed to be the name of an actual London tavern keeper, but emendations have been suggested by various editors; **stoup:** cup or tankard.

61-4, 71-4. **In youth . . . :** the clown's recollection of a contemporary poem printed in Richard Tottel's *Miscellany* (1557) and attributed to Lord Vaux

63. **contract:** shorten; **behove:** benefit

67-8. **Custom hath made it in him a property of easiness:** custom has made him easy in it.

69-70. **hath the daintier sense:** is more sensitive

73. **shipped me intil the land:** returned me to the dust

*Clown.* Ay, tell me that, and unyoke.
*Other.* Marry, now I can tell!
*Clown.* To't.
*Other.* Mass, I cannot tell.                                          55

Enter *Hamlet* and *Horatio* afar off.

*Clown.* Cudgel thy brains no more about it, for your
dull ass will not mend his pace with beating; and when
you are asked this question next, say "a grave-maker."
The houses he makes lasts till doomsday. Go, get thee to
Yaughan; fetch me a stoup of liquor.                                   60
                                        [*Exit Second Clown.*]

[*Clown digs and*] sings.

*In youth when I did love, did love,*
  *Methought it was very sweet;*
*To contract—O—the time for—a—my behove,*
  *O, methought there—a—was nothing—a—meet.*

*Ham.* Has this fellow no feeling of his business, that he    65
sings at grave-making?
*Hor.* Custom hath made it in him a property of easiness.
*Ham.* 'Tis e'en so. The hand of little employment hath
the daintier sense.                                                    70
*Clown.* (*Sings*)

    *But age with his stealing steps*
      *Hath clawed me in his clutch,*
    *And hath shipped me intil the land,*
      *As if I had never been such.*
                                        [*Throws up a skull.*]

76. **jowls:** knocks

78. **o'erreaches:** gets the better of

86-7. **chapless:** without a lower jaw; **mazzard:** head, a slang term

90. **loggets:** a game played with pieces of wood

96. **quiddities:** logical subtleties; **quillets:** quibbles

98. **sconce:** head

101-2. **his statutes, his recognizances . . . :** Hamlet is using legal verbiage with punning effect to emphasize the irony of the macabre situation.

*Ham.* That skull had a tongue in it, and could sing 75
once. How the knave jowls it to the ground, as if 'twere
Cain's jawbone, that did the first murder! This might be
the pate of a politician, which this ass now o'erreaches;
one that would circumvent God, might it not?

*Hor.* It might, my lord. 80

*Ham.* Or of a courtier, which could say "Good morrow,
sweet lord! How dost thou, good lord?" This might be my
Lord Such-a-one, that praised my Lord Such-a-one's horse
when he meant to beg it—might it not?

*Hor.* Ay, my lord. 85

*Ham.* Why, e'en so! and now my Lady Worm's, chapless, and knocked about the mazzard with a sexton's
spade. Here's fine revolution, if we had the trick to see't.
Did these bones cost no more the breeding but to play at
loggets with 'em? Mine ache to think on't. 90

*Clown. (Sings)*

> *A pickaxe and a spade, a spade,*
> *For and a shrouding sheet;*
> *O, a pit of clay for to be made*
> *For such a guest is meet.*
> [*Throws up another skull.*]

*Ham.* There's another. Why may not that be the skull 95
of a lawyer? Where be his quiddities now, his quillets,
his cases, his tenures, and his tricks? Why does he suffer
this rude knave now to knock him about the sconce with
a dirty shovel, and will not tell him of his action of bat-
tery? Hum! This fellow might be in's time a great buyer 100
of land, with his statutes, his recognizances, his fines, his
double vouchers, his recoveries. Is this the fine of his
fines, and the recovery of his recoveries, to have his fine

106. **indentures**: conveyances or contracts, prepared in pairs

107. **conveyances**: deeds

122. **quick**: living

132. **absolute**: positive, precise

132-33. **by the card**: to the point, as by a compass

133. **equivocation**: a term in logic meaning a fallacy resulting from the use of language that can be understood two ways

pate full of fine dirt? Will his vouchers vouch him no
more of his purchases, and double ones too, than the 105
length and breadth of a pair of indentures? The very
conveyances of his lands will scarcely lie in this box; and
must the inheritor himself have no more, ha?

*Hor.* Not a jot more, my lord.

*Ham.* Is not parchment made of sheepskins? 110

*Hor.* Ay, my lord, and of calveskins too.

*Ham.* They are sheep and calves which seek out assurance in that. I will speak to this fellow. Whose grave's
this, sirrah?

*Clown.* Mine, sir. 115

> [*Sings*] *O, a pit of clay for to be made*
> *For such a guest is meet.*

*Ham.* I think it be thine indeed, for thou liest in't.

*Clown.* You lie out on't, sir, and therefore 'tis not yours.
For my part, I do not lie in't, yet it is mine. 120

*Ham.* Thou dost lie in't, to be in't and say it is thine.
'Tis for the dead, not for the quick; therefore thou liest.

*Clown.* 'Tis a quick lie, sir; 'twill away again from me
to you.

*Ham.* What man dost thou dig it for? 125

*Clown.* For no man, sir.

*Ham.* What woman then?

*Clown.* For none neither.

*Ham.* Who is to be buried in't?

*Clown.* One that was a woman, sir; but, rest her soul, 130
she's dead.

*Ham.* How absolute the knave is! We must speak by
the card, or equivocation will undo us. By the Lord,

135. **picked:** refined

136. **kibe:** chilblain. The age is so refined that peasants follow at the very heels of courtiers in elegance.

159. **pocky:** diseased

Horatio, this three years I have taken note of it, the age
is grown so picked that the toe of the peasant comes so  135
near the heel of the courtier he galls his kibe.—How long
hast thou been a grave-maker?

  *Clown.* Of all the days i' the year, I came to't that day
that our last king Hamlet overcame Fortinbras.

  *Ham.* How long is that since?                             140

  *Clown.* Cannot you tell that? Every fool can tell that.
It was the very day that young Hamlet was born—he that
is mad, and sent into England.

  *Ham.* Ay, marry, why was he sent into England?

  *Clown.* Why, because he was mad. He shall recover  145
his wits there; or, if he do not, 'tis no great matter there.

  *Ham.* Why?

  *Clown.* 'Twill not be seen in him there. There the
men are as mad as he.

  *Ham.* How came he mad?                                    150

  *Clown.* Very strangely, they say.

  *Ham.* How strangely?

  *Clown.* Faith, e'en with losing his wits.

  *Ham.* Upon what ground?

  *Clown.* Why, here in Denmark. I have been sexton  155
here, man and boy, thirty years.

  *Ham.* How long will a man lie i' the earth ere he rot?

  *Clown.* Faith, if he be not rotten before he die (as we
have many pocky corses now-a-days that will scarce hold
the laying in), he will last you some eight year or nine  160
year. A tanner will last you nine year.

  *Ham.* Why he more than another?

  *Clown.* Why, sir, his hide is so tanned with his trade
that he will keep out water a great while; and your

165. **sore**: grievous; **whoreson**: a term of jocular abuse

185. **chapfall'n**: chinless

187. **favor**: facial appearance

Yorick, the King's jester.
From Olaus Magnus, *Historia de gentibus septentrionalibus* (1555).

water is a sore decayer of your whoreson dead body. 165
Here's a skull now: this skull hath lien i' the earth three-
and-twenty years.

*Ham.* Whose was it?

*Clown.* A whoreson mad fellow's it was. Whose do
you think it was? 170

*Ham.* Nay, I know not.

*Clown.* A pestilence on him for a mad rogue! He
poured a flagon of Rhenish on my head once. This same
skull, sir, was Yorick's skull, the King's jester.

*Ham.* This? 175

*Clown.* E'en that.

*Ham.* Let me see. [*Takes the skull.*] Alas, poor Yorick!
I knew him, Horatio. A fellow of infinite jest, of most excellent fancy. He hath borne me on his back a thousand
times. And now how abhorred in my imagination it is! 180
My gorge rises at it. Here hung those lips that I have kissed
I know not how oft. Where be your gibes now? your
gambols? your songs? your flashes of merriment that were
wont to set the table on a roar? Not one now, to mock
your own grinning? Quite chapfall'n? Now get you to 185
my lady's chamber, and tell her, let her paint an inch
thick, to this favor she must come. Make her laugh at
that. Prithee, Horatio, tell me one thing.

*Hor.* What's that, my lord?

*Ham.* Dost thou think Alexander looked o' this fashion 190
i' the earth?

*Hor.* E'en so.

*Ham.* And smelt so? Pah!  [*Puts down the skull.*]

*Hor.* E'en so, my lord.

*Ham.* To what base uses we may return, Horatio! Why 195

198. **curiously**: ingeniously
208. **flaw**: gust of wind
213. **Fordo**: destroy; see II. [i.] 114; **it**: its.
214. **Couch**: hide

may not imagination trace the noble dust of Alexander
till he find it stopping a bunghole?

*Hor.* 'Twere to consider too curiously, to consider so.

*Ham.* No, faith, not a jot; but to follow him thither
with modesty enough, and likelihood to lead it; as thus: 200
Alexander died, Alexander was buried, Alexander re-
turneth into dust; the dust is earth; of earth we make
loam; and why of that loam (whereto he was converted)
might they not stop a beer barrel?

> Imperious Cæsar, dead and turned to clay, 205
> Might stop a hole to keep the wind away.
> O, that that earth which kept the world in awe
> Should patch a wall t' expel the winter's flaw!

But soft! but soft! aside! Here comes the King—

*Enter King, Queen, Laertes, and a coffin, with
[Priests and] Lords attendant.*

> The Queen, the courtiers. Who is this they follow? 210
> And with such maimed rites? This doth betoken
> The corse they follow did with desp'rate hand
> Fordo it own life. 'Twas of some estate.
> Couch we awhile, and mark.

> > *[Retires with Horatio.]*

*Laer.* What ceremony else? 215

*Ham.* That is Laertes,
A very noble youth. Mark.

*Laer.* What ceremony else?

*Priest.* Her obsequies have been as far enlarged
As we have warranty. Her death was doubtful; 220
And, but that great command o'ersways the order,
She should in ground unsanctified have lodged

224. **Shards:** broken pieces of pottery

225. **crants:** garlands, from the German *kranz.* These were the usual accompaniment of the funerals of unmarried girls.

232. **peace-parted souls:** souls departed in peace

237. **howling:** that is, in hell

245. **ingenious sense:** finely tuned mental faculties

250. **Pelion:** a high mountain which the giants of Greek mythology piled on Mount Ossa in an effort to reach Olympus

Till the last trumpet. For charitable prayers,
Shards, flints, and pebbles should be thrown on her.
Yet here she is allowed her virgin crants, 225
Her maiden strewments, and the bringing home
Of bell and burial.
    *Laer.* Must there no more be done?
    *Priest.*                    No more be done.
We should profane the service of the dead 230
To sing a requiem and such rest to her
As to peace-parted souls.
    *Laer.*            Lay her i' the earth,
And from her fair and unpolluted flesh
May violets spring! I tell thee, churlish priest, 235
A minist'ring angel shall my sister be
When thou liest howling.
    *Ham.*            What, the fair Ophelia?
    *Queen.* Sweets to the sweet! Farewell.
                             *[Scatters flowers.]*
I hoped thou shouldst have been my Hamlet's wife; 240
I thought thy bride-bed to have decked, sweet maid,
And not have strewed thy grave.
    *Laer.*               O, treble woe
Fall ten times treble on that cursed head
Whose wicked deed thy most ingenious sense
Deprived thee of! Hold off the earth awhile, 245
Till I have caught her once more in mine arms.
                         *Leaps in the grave.*
Now pile your dust upon the quick and dead
Till of this flat a mountain you have made
T' o'ertop old Pelion or the skyish head 250
Of blue Olympus.
    *Ham.* *[Advancing]* What is he whose grief

260. **splenitive**: synonymous with **rash**

274. **forbear him**: leave him alone.

275. **thou't**: thou wilt

276. **Woo't**: will you

277. **eisell**: vinegar, the drinking of which was supposed to heighten grief

280. **quick**: alive; see V. [i.] 122.

Bears such an emphasis? whose phrase of sorrow
Conjures the wand'ring stars, and makes them stand
Like wonder-wounded hearers? This is I,                    255
Hamlet the Dane.                    [*Leaps in after Laertes.*]
    *Laer.*          The devil take thy soul!
                              [*Grappling with him.*]
    *Ham.* Thou pray'st not well.
I prithee take thy fingers from my throat;
For, though I am not splenitive and rash,                  260
Yet have I in me something dangerous,
Which let thy wisdom fear. Hold off thy hand!
    *King.* Pluck them asunder.
    *Queen.*               Hamlet, Hamlet!
    *All.* Gentlemen!                                      265
    *Hor.*          Good my lord, be quiet.
        [*Attendants part them, and they leave the grave.*]
    *Ham.* Why, I will fight with him upon this theme
Until my eyelids will no longer wag.
    *Queen.* O my son, what theme?
    *Ham.* I loved Ophelia. Forty thousand brothers        270
Could not (with all their quantity of love)
Make up my sum. What wilt thou do for her?
    *King.* O, he is mad, Laertes.
    *Queen.* For love of God, forbear him!
    *Ham.* 'Swounds, show me what thou't do.               275
Woo't weep? woo't fight? woo't fast? woo't tear thyself?
Woo't drink up eisell? eat a crocodile?
I'll do't. Dost thou come here to whine?
To outface me with leaping in her grave?
Be buried quick with her, and so will I.                   280
And if thou prate of mountains, let them throw
Millions of acres on us, till our ground,

283. **the burning zone:** the belt between the tropics of Cancer and Capricorn

289. **golden couplets:** the two young of each brood, which are covered with yellow down

297. **in:** with

299. **the present push:** immediate execution

Singeing his pate against the burning zone,
Make Ossa like a wart! Nay, an thou'lt mouth,
I'll rant as well as thou.                                    285

    *Queen.*           This is mere madness;
And thus a while the fit will work on him.
Anon, as patient as the female dove
When that her golden couplets are disclosed,
His silence will sit drooping.                              290

    *Ham.*           Hear you, sir!
What is the reason that you use me thus?
I loved you ever. But it is no matter.
Let Hercules himself do what he may,
The cat will mew, and dog will have his day.   *Exit.* 295

    *King.* I pray thee, good Horatio, wait upon him.

                             *Exit Horatio.*
[*To Laertes*] Strengthen your patience in our last night's
    speech.
We'll put the matter to the present push.—
Good Gertrude, set some watch over your son.—      300
This grave shall have a living monument.
An hour of quiet shortly shall we see;
Till then in patience our proceeding be.

                             *Exeunt.*

**V. [ii.]** Hamlet relates the details of his escape and the fatal outcome for Rosencrantz and Guildenstern. Osric enters to inform Hamlet that Claudius is wagering upon his skill at fencing against that of Laertes. After a wit contest with the foppish courtier, Hamlet agrees to the match. To Horatio he confides a certain foreboding, but he is fatalistic, and Horatio's own pessimism cannot move him to excuse himself.

After exchanges of courtesy with Laertes, the match begins. Hamlet has scored two hits when his mother drinks to his health from the poisoned cup. Laertes, desperate, catches Hamlet off guard and pricks him with the poisoned rapier. Hamlet's anger is aroused and he manages to exchange weapons with Laertes and to wound him. The Queen dies and Laertes clears his conscience before his own death by revealing the whole plot. Hamlet leaps at Claudius and runs him through, and makes sure of his death by forcing him to drink the poisoned liquor. Before he dies, Hamlet insists that Horatio live on to tell the whole story, and names Fortinbras, whose army is heard in the distance, as successor to the Danish throne.

⟪▮▮▮▮▮▮▮▮▮▮▮▮▮▮▮▮▮▮▮▮▮▮▮▮▮▮▮▮▮▮▮⟫

7. **mutines:** mutineers; **bilboes:** ship's stocks for confining prisoners
10. **pall:** fail
21. **exact:** strict
22. **Larded:** filled out

24, 25: see next page.

[Scene II. The same. A hall in the Castle.]

Enter *Hamlet* and *Horatio.*

*Ham.* So much for this, sir; now shall you see the
    other.
You do remember all the circumstance?
  *Hor.* Remember it, my lord!
  *Ham.* Sir, in my heart there was a kind of fighting    5
That would not let me sleep. Methought I lay
Worse than the mutines in the bilboes. Rashly—
And praised be rashness for it; let us know,
Our indiscretion sometime serves us well
When our deep plots do pall; and that should learn us   10
There's a divinity that shapes our ends,
Rough-hew them how we will—
  *Hor.*                That is most certain.
  *Ham.* Up from my cabin,
My sea-gown scarfed about me, in the dark     15
Groped I to find out them; had my desire,
Fingered their packet, and in fine withdrew
To mine own room again; making so bold
(My fears forgetting manners) to unseal
Their grand commission; where I found, Horatio   20
(O royal knavery!), an exact command,
Larded with many several sorts of reasons,
Importing Denmark's health, and England's too,
With, ho! such bugs and goblins in my life—
That, on the supervise, no leisure bated,     25
No, not to stay the grinding of the axe,
My head should be struck off.

24. **such bugs and goblins in my life:** such terrifying dangers in my continued existence; **bugs:** ghosts, a word which survives in modern usage only in "bugaboo"

25. **on the supervise, no leisure bated:** on looking over the instruction, no time should be wasted.

33-4. **Ere I could make a prologue to my brains,/ They had begun the play:** almost instinctively my mind began to work.

35. **fair:** in the beautiful hand of a professional clerk

36. **statists:** statesmen

39. **yeoman's:** dependable and substantial. The sturdy qualities of the English yeomanry were proverbial.

40. **effect:** tenor, meaning

46. **stand a comma 'tween their amities:** the comma acts as a connector, hence Peace is pictured as reinforcing their mutual friendship.

51. **shriving:** confession and absolution

53. **ordinant:** effective

58. **changeling:** exchange

*Hor.* Is't possible?

*Ham.* Here's the commission; read it at more leisure.
But wilt thou hear me how I did proceed?                    30
*Hor.* I beseech you.
*Ham.* Being thus benetted round with villainies,
Ere I could make a prologue to my brains,
They had begun the play. I sat me down;
Devised a new commission; wrote it fair.                    35
I once did hold it, as our statists do,
A baseness to write fair, and labored much
How to forget that learning; but, sir, now
It did me yeoman's service. Wilt thou know
The effect of what I wrote?                                 40
*Hor.* Ay, good my lord.
*Ham.* An earnest conjuration from the King,
As England was his faithful tributary,
As love between them like the palm might flourish,
As peace should still her wheaten garland wear             45
And stand a comma 'tween their amities,
And many such-like as's of great charge,
That, on the view and knowing of these contents,
Without debatement further, more or less,
He should the bearers put to sudden death,                 50
Not shriving time allowed.
*Hor.* How was this sealed?
*Ham.* Why, even in that was heaven ordinant.
I had my father's signet in my purse,
Which was the model of that Danish seal;                   55
Folded the writ up in the form of the other,
Subscribed it, gave't the impression, placed it safely,
The changeling never known. Now, the next day

61. **to't**: to death

64. **defeat**: destruction; see II. ii. 578.

65. **insinuation**: winding into the affair; that is, interference

67. **pass**: thrust; see IV. [vii.] 153; **fell**: deadly; see II. ii. 480.

70. **Does it not . . . stand me now upon**: is it not now my obligation

72. **election**: Claudius was chosen by the Danes to assume the throne.

73. **proper**: own

74. **coz'nage**: trickery; see **cozened**, III. [iv.] 87.

75. **quit**: repay, finish

77. **In**: into

86. **bravery**: ostentation

Was our sea-fight; and what to this was sequent
Thou know'st already.　　　　　　　　　　　　　　　　60

　　*Hor.* So Guildenstern and Rosencrantz go to't.

　　*Ham.* Why, man, they did make love to this employ-
　　　ment!

They are not near my conscience; their defeat
Does by their own insinuation grow.　　　　　　　　　65
'Tis dangerous when the baser nature comes
Between the pass and fell incensed points
Of mighty opposites.

　　*Hor.*　　　　　　　Why, what a king is this!

　　*Ham.* Does it not, think'st thee, stand me now upon—　70
He that hath killed my king, and whored my mother;
Popped in between the election and my hopes;
Thrown out his angle for my proper life,
And with such coz'nage—is't not perfect conscience
To quit him with this arm? And is't not to be damned　75
To let this canker of our nature come
In further evil?

　　*Hor.* It must be shortly known to him from England
What is the issue of the business there.

　　*Ham.* It will be short; the interim is mine,　　　　80
And a man's life 's no more than to say "one."
But I am very sorry, good Horatio,
That to Laertes I forgot myself;
For by the image of my cause I see
The portraiture of his. I'll court his favors.　　　　85
But sure the bravery of his grief did put me
Into a tow'ring passion.

　　*Hor.*　　　　　　　Peace! Who comes here?

91. **waterfly:** a showy trifler

93-4. **gracious:** virtuous

95-6. **Let a beast be lord of beasts, and his crib shall stand at the king's mess:** if an ass is only wealthy enough, he can gain admittance to the court.

96. **chough:** a bird noted for its noisy chatter

101. **Put your bonnet to his right use:** that is, put on your hat. Hats were commonly worn indoors but were doffed in courtesy in the presence of superiors.

105. **indifferent:** somewhat; see II. ii. 244.

107. **complexion:** temperament

113. **for mine ease:** the conventional polite phrase of protest when urged to put on one's hat

115. **absolute:** complete; **differences:** accomplishments that set him apart

116. **soft society:** gentle and courteous manners; **great showing:** noble appearance

*Enter young Osric, a courtier.*

*Osr.* Your lordship is right welcome back to Denmark.

*Ham.* I humbly thank you, sir. [*Aside to Horatio*] Dost 90
know this waterfly?

*Hor.* [*Aside to Hamlet*] No, my good lord.

*Ham.* [*Aside to Horatio*] Thy state is the more gracious; for 'tis a vice to know him. He hath much land, and
fertile. Let a beast be lord of beasts, and his crib shall 95
stand at the king's mess. 'Tis a chough; but, as I say,
spacious in the possession of dirt.

*Osr.* Sweet lord, if your lordship were at leisure, I
should impart a thing to you from his Majesty.

*Ham.* I will receive it, sir, with all diligence of spirit. 100
Put your bonnet to his right use, 'tis for the head.

*Osr.* I thank your lordship, it is very hot.

*Ham.* No, believe me, 'tis very cold; the wind is northerly.

*Osr.* It is indifferent cold, my lord, indeed. 105

*Ham.* But yet methinks it is very sultry and hot for my
complexion.

*Osr.* Exceedingly, my lord; it is very sultry, as 'twere—
I cannot tell how. But, my lord, his Majesty bade me signify to you that he has laid a great wager on your head. 110
Sir, this is the matter—

*Ham.* I beseech you remember.
[*Hamlet moves him to put on his hat.*]

*Osr.* Nay, good my lord; for mine ease, in good faith.
Sir, here is newly come to court Laertes; believe me, an
absolute gentleman, full of most excellent differences, of 115
very soft society and great showing. Indeed, to speak

117. **feelingly:** perceptively, with true awareness of his worth; **the card or calendar of gentry:** a veritable handbook of courtesy

118-19. **the continent of what part a gentleman would see:** the possessor of exactly the qualities one gentleman expects another to have

120. **perdition:** loss

121-23. **to divide him inventorially would dozy the arithmetic of memory, and yet but yaw neither in respect of his quick sail:** one would be dizzied by an effort to inventory his qualities before even coming close to accuracy; **dozy:** dizzy, confuse; **yaw:** veer back and forth off the course.

124. **great article:** many excellencies; **infusion:** the character with which he is infused

126. **his semblable is his mirror:** his true image can be found only in his own reflection.

126-27. **who else would trace him, his umbrage:** anyone else seeking to emulate him would achieve only a shadowy similarity.

129-30. **concernancy:** relevance; **wrap the gentleman in our more rawer breath:** that is, encompass him with our words, which do not match him in fineness

133. **do't:** outdo Osric in extravagant affectation of language

134. **nomination:** naming

140-41. **I would you did . . . if you did, it would not much approve me:** I would prefer you not to
[continued

145-46, 147: see next page.

137

feelingly of him, he is the card or calendar of gentry; for
you shall find in him the continent of what part a gentleman would see.

*Ham.* Sir, his definement suffers no perdition in you; 120
though, I know, to divide him inventorially would dozy
the arithmetic of memory, and yet but yaw neither in respect of his quick sail. But, in the verity of extolment, I
take him to be a soul of great article, and his infusion of
such dearth and rareness as, to make true diction of him, 125
his semblable is his mirror, and who else would trace him,
his umbrage, nothing more.

*Osr.* Your lordship speaks most infallibly of him.

*Ham.* The concernancy, sir? Why do we wrap the
gentleman in our more rawer breath? 130

*Osr.* Sir?

*Hor.* [*Aside to Hamlet*] Is't not possible to understand
in another tongue? You will do't, sir, really.

*Ham.* What imports the nomination of this gentleman?

*Osr.* Of Laertes? 135

*Hor.* [*Aside*] His purse is empty already; all's golden
words are spent.

*Ham.* Of him, sir.

*Osr.* I know you are not ignorant—

*Ham.* I would you did, sir; yet, in faith, if you did, it 140
would not much approve me. Well, sir?

*Osr.* You are not ignorant of what excellence Laertes
is—

*Ham.* I dare not confess that, lest I should compare
with him in excellence; but to know a man well were to 145
know himself.

*Osr.* I mean, sir, for his weapon; but in the imputation
laid on him by them, in his meed he's unfellowed.

think me ignorant, but if you should so judge me, your approval would have little weight; **approve:** commend.

145-46. **to know a man well were to know himself:** to judge another properly requires complete self-knowledge.

147. **imputation:** reputation

148. **them:** his weapons; **meed:** merits; **unfellowed:** unmatched

153. **imponed:** staked

154-55. **poniards:** daggers; **assigns:** accessories; **girdle, hangers:** sword belt and its attaching straps

156. **dear to fancy:** tastefully designed; **responsive:** corresponding in design

157. **liberal conceit:** imaginative pattern

160. **margent:** marginal comment

168. **laid:** bet

170. **twelve for nine:** the exact meaning of this has baffled all commentators. Apparently this talk concerning the wager represents fencing jargon of the time.

171-72. **the answer:** that is, to answer the challenge

*Ham.* What's his weapon?

*Osr.* Rapier and dagger. 150

*Ham.* That's two of his weapons—but well.

*Osr.* The King, sir, hath wagered with him six Barbary horses; against the which he has imponed, as I take it, six French rapiers and poniards, with their assigns, as girdle, hangers, and so. Three of the carriages, in faith, are very 155 dear to fancy, very responsive to the hilts, most delicate carriages, and of very liberal conceit.

*Ham.* What call you the carriages?

*Hor.* [*Aside to Hamlet*] I knew you must be edified by the margent ere you had done. 160

*Osr.* The carriages, sir, are the hangers.

*Ham.* The phrase would be more germane to the matter if we could carry cannon by our sides. I would it might be hangers till then. But on! Six Barbary horses against six French swords, their assigns, and three liberal-con- 165 ceited carriages: that's the French bet against the Danish. Why is this all imponed, as you call it?

*Osr.* The King, sir, hath laid that, in a dozen passes between yourself and him, he shall not exceed you three hits; he hath laid on twelve for nine, and it would come 170 to immediate trial if your lordship would vouchsafe the answer.

*Ham.* How if I answer no?

*Osr.* I mean, my lord, the opposition of your person in trial. 175

*Ham.* Sir, I will walk here in the hall. If it please his Majesty, it is the breathing time of day with me. Let the foils be brought, the gentleman willing, and the King hold his purpose, I will win for him if I can; if not, I will gain nothing but my shame and the odd hits. 180

186. **for's turn:** to perform his service

187-88. **this lapwing runs away with the shell upon his head:** this upstart is as precocious as the lapwing, which runs away when it is barely hatched. Osric apparently has finally donned his hat.

189. **comply with:** observe proper courtesy toward; see II. ii. 382.

191. **drossy:** worthless

192. **outward habit of encounter:** superficial clothing of social grace; **yeasty:** frothy, without substance

193-94. **carries them through and through the most fanned and winnowed opinions:** that is, their elegant manners gain the approval of the most discriminating. **Fanned** and **winnowed** are synonymous for "sifted, refined." The First Folio reads "fond" for **fanned,** and the Second Quarto reads "prophane and trennowed." **Fanned** was suggested by the eighteenth-century editor William Warburton.

204. **In happy time:** opportunely

205-6. **use some gentle entertainment to:** greet with friendly courtesy

*Osr.* Shall I redeliver you e'en so?

*Ham.* To this effect, sir, after what flourish your nature will.

*Osr.* I commend my duty to your lordship.

*Ham.* Yours, yours. [*Exit Osric.*] He does well to com- 185
mend it himself; there are no tongues else for's turn.

*Hor.* This lapwing runs away with the shell on his head.

*Ham.* He did comply with his dug before he sucked it.
Thus has he, and many more of the same bevy that I 190
know the drossy age dotes on, only got the tune of the
time and outward habit of encounter—a kind of yeasty
collection, which carries them through and through the
most fanned and winnowed opinions; and do but blow
them to their trial—the bubbles are out. 195

Enter a *Lord.*

*Lord.* My lord, his Majesty commended him to you by
young Osric, who brings back to him, that you attend
him in the hall. He sends to know if your pleasure hold to
play with Laertes, or that you will take longer time.

*Ham.* I am constant to my purposes; they follow the 200
King's pleasure. If his fitness speaks, mine is ready; now
or whensoever, provided I be so able as now.

*Lord.* The King and Queen and all are coming down.

*Ham.* In happy time.

*Lord.* The Queen desires you to use some gentle enter- 205
tainment to Laertes before you fall to play.

*Ham.* She well instructs me.

[*Exit Lord.*]

*Hor.* You will lose this wager, my lord.

A gentleman of the time of James I dressed for sport.
From the Trevelyon MS. (c. 1608).

**210. at the odds:** with the advantage allowed me

**214-15. gaingiving:** misgiving

**217. repair:** coming

**221-22. Since no man has aught of what he leaves, what is't to leave betimes:** since all we really possess are our endowments of personality and spirit, what does it matter when we leave the world.

**223. Let be:** let the matter pass.

**229. This presence:** this royal audience

*Ham.* I do not think so. Since he went into France I
have been in continual practice; I shall win at the odds. 210
But thou wouldst not think how ill all's here about my
heart. But it is no matter.

*Hor.* Nay, good my lord—

*Ham.* It is but foolery; but it is such a kind of gaingiving as would perhaps trouble a woman. 215

*Hor.* If your mind dislike anything, obey it. I will forestall their repair hither and say you are not fit.

*Ham.* Not a whit, we defy augury; there's a special
providence in the fall of a sparrow. If it be now, 'tis not
to come; if it be not to come, it will be now; if it be not 220
now, yet it will come: the readiness is all. Since no man
has aught of what he leaves, what is't to leave betimes?
Let be.

*Enter* King, Queen, Laertes, [Osric], *and* Lords, *with
other* Attendants *with foils and gauntlets. A table and
flagons of wine on it.*

*King.* Come, Hamlet, come, and take this hand from
me. 225

        *[He puts Laertes' hand into Hamlet's.]*

*Ham.* Give me your pardon, sir. I have done you
    wrong;

But pardon't, as you are a gentleman.

This presence knows,

And you must needs have heard, how I am punished 230

With sore distraction. What I have done

That might your nature, honor, and exception

Roughly awake, I here proclaim was madness.

Was't Hamlet wronged Laertes? Never Hamlet.

246. **in nature:** insofar as my personal feelings are concerned

251. **voice:** authority

252. **ungored:** unmarred

259. **foil:** Hamlet is punning on the other meaning of **foil:** a contrast to Laertes' brilliance.

261. **Stick fiery off:** stand out brightly

If Hamlet from himself be ta'en away,                    235
And when he's not himself does wrong Laertes,
Then Hamlet does it not, Hamlet denies it.
Who does it, then? His madness. If't be so,
Hamlet is of the faction that is wronged;
His madness is poor Hamlet's enemy.                    240
Sir, in this audience,
Let my disclaiming from a purposed evil
Free me so far in your most generous thoughts
That I have shot my arrow o'er the house
And hurt my brother.                    245
   *Laer.*          I am satisfied in nature,
Whose motive in this case should stir me most
To my revenge. But in my terms of honor
I stand aloof, and will no reconcilement
Till by some elder masters of known honor                    250
I have a voice and precedent of peace
To keep my name ungored. But till that time
I do receive your offered love like love,
And will not wrong it.
   *Ham.*          I embrace it freely,                    255
And will this brother's wager frankly play.
Give us the foils. Come on.
   *Laer.*          Come, one for me.
   *Ham.* I'll be your foil, Laertes. In mine ignorance
Your skill shall, like a star i' the darkest night,                    260
Stick fiery off indeed.
   *Laer.*          You mock me, sir.
   *Ham.* No, by this hand.
   *King.* Give them the foils, young Osric. Cousin Hamlet,
You know the wager?                    265

269. **is bettered:** has improved

271. **likes:** pleases; see II. ii. 85; **have all a length:** are all the same length

275. **quit in answer of the third exchange:** repay Laertes' previous hits in the third bout

278. **union:** a large pearl

*Ham.*                Very well, my lord.
Your Grace has laid the odds o' the weaker side.

*King.* I do not fear it, I have seen you both;
But since he is bettered, we have therefore odds.

*Laer.* This is too heavy; let me see another.                    270

*Ham.* This likes me well. These foils have all a length?
                                        *Prepare to play.*

*Osr.* Ay, my good lord.

*King.* Set me the stoups of wine upon that table.
If Hamlet give the first or second hit,
Or quit in answer of the third exchange,                          275
Let all the battlements their ordnance fire;
The King shall drink to Hamlet's better breath,
And in the cup an union shall he throw
Richer than that which four successive kings
In Denmark's crown have worn. Give me the cups;                   280
And let the kettle to the trumpet speak,
The trumpet to the cannoneer without,
The cannons to the heavens, the heaven to earth,
"Now the King drinks to Hamlet." Come, begin.
And you the judges, bear a wary eye.                              285

*Ham.* Come on, sir.

*Laer.*                Come, my lord.        *They play.*

*Ham.*                        One.

*Laer.*                        No.

*Ham.*                        Judgment!       290

*Osr.* A hit, a very palpable hit.

*Laer.*                    Well, again!

*King.* Stay, give me drink. Hamlet, this pearl is thine;
Here's to thy health.
            *Drum; trumpets sound; a piece goes off [within].*
                    Give him the cup.                              295

300. **fat:** probably "out of training"
301. **napkin:** handkerchief
315. **make a wanton of me:** toy with me

*Ham.* I'll play this bout first; set it by awhile.
Come. (*They play.*) Another hit. What say you?

*Laer.* A touch, a touch; I do confess.

*King.* Our son shall win.

*Queen.*                    He's fat, and scant of breath.  300
Here, Hamlet, take my napkin, rub thy brows.
The Queen carouses to thy fortune, Hamlet.

*Ham.* Good madam!

*King.*                    Gertrude, do not drink.

*Queen.* I will, my lord; I pray you pardon me.          305
                                        [*Drinks.*]

*King.* [*Aside*] It is the poisoned cup; it is too late.

*Ham.* I dare not drink yet, madam; by-and-by.

*Queen.* Come, let me wipe thy face.

*Laer.* My lord, I'll hit him now.

*King.*                    I do not think't.              310

*Laer.* [*Aside*] And yet it is almost against my conscience.

*Ham.* Come for the third, Laertes! You but dally;
I pray you pass with your best violence;
I am afeard you make a wanton of me.                     315

*Laer.* Say you so? Come on.                    *Play.*

*Osr.* Nothing neither way.

*Laer.* Have at you now!

    [*Laertes wounds Hamlet; then,*] *in scuffling, they
        change rapiers,* [*and Hamlet wounds Laertes*].

*King.*                    Part them! They are incensed.

*Ham.* Nay come! again!                                  320
                            [*The Queen falls.*]

*Osr.*                    Look to the Queen there, ho!

*Hor.* They bleed on both sides. How is it, my lord?

*Osr.* How is't, Laertes?

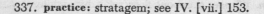

**337. practice:** stratagem; see IV. [vii.] 153.

Climax of the duel.

From Henry de Saint Didier, *Traicte contenant les secrets du premier livre sur l'espee seule* . . . (1573).

*Laer.* Why, as a woodcock to mine own springe, Osric.
I am justly killed with mine own treachery.　　325
　*Ham.* How does the Queen?
　*King.*　　　　　　She swoons to see them bleed.
　*Queen.* No, no! the drink, the drink! O my dear Ham-
　　let!
The drink, the drink! I am poisoned.　　　[*Dies.*] 330
　*Ham.* O villainy! Ho! let the door be locked.
Treachery! Seek it out.

　　　　　　　　　　　　[*Laertes falls.*]

　*Laer.* It is here, Hamlet. Hamlet, thou art slain;
No med'cine in the world can do thee good.
In thee there is not half an hour of life.　　335
The treacherous instrument is in thy hand,
Unbated and envenomed. The foul practice
Hath turned itself on me. Lo, here I lie,
Never to rise again. Thy mother's poisoned.
I can no more. The King, the King's to blame.　　340
　*Ham.* The point envenomed too?
Then, venom, to thy work.　　　　*Hurts the King.*
　*All.* Treason! treason!
　*King.* O, yet defend me, friends! I am but hurt.
　*Ham.* Here, thou incestuous, murd'rous, damned Dane, 345
Drink off this potion! Is thy union here?
Follow my mother.

　　　　　　　　　　　　*King dies.*

　*Laer.*　　　　He is justly served.
It is a poison tempered by himself.
Exchange forgiveness with me, noble Hamlet.　　350
Mine and my father's death come not upon thee,
Nor thine on me!　　　　　　　*Dies.*
　*Ham.* Heaven make thee free of it! I follow thee.

384. **solicited:** evoked, brought about (these happenings)

I am dead, Horatio. Wretched queen, adieu!
You that look pale and tremble at this chance,        355
That are but mutes or audience to this act,
Had I but time (as this fell sergeant, Death,
Is strict in his arrest) O, I could tell you—
But let it be. Horatio, I am dead;
Thou liv'st; report me and my cause aright        300
To the unsatisfied.
   *Hor.*        Never believe it.
I am more an antique Roman than a Dane.
Here's yet some liquor left.
   *Ham.*        As th'art a man,        365
Give me the cup. Let go! By heaven, I'll have't.
O good Horatio, what a wounded name
(Things standing thus unknown) shall live behind me!
If thou didst ever hold me in thy heart,
Absent thee from felicity awhile,        370
And in this harsh world draw thy breath in pain,
To tell my story.        *March afar off, and shot within.*
        What warlike noise is this?
   *Osr.* Young Fortinbras, with conquest come from
     Poland,        375
To the ambassadors of England gives
This warlike volley.
   *Ham.*        O, I die, Horatio!
The potent poison quite o'ercrows my spirit.
I cannot live to hear the news from England,        380
But I do prophesy the election lights
On Fortinbras. He has my dying voice.
So tell him, with th' occurrents, more and less,
Which have solicited—the rest is silence.        *Dies.*

**392. This quarry cries on havoc:** this heap of dead announces indiscriminate slaughter.

**405. jump:** exactly: see I. i. 77.

**408. stage:** platform

*Hor.* Now cracks a noble heart. Good night, sweet  385
   prince,
And flights of angels sing thee to thy rest!
                              [*March within.*]
Why does the drum come hither?

Enter *Fortinbras* and *English Ambassadors,* with *Drum,*
          *Colors,* and *Attendants.*

*Fort.* Where is this sight?
*Hor.*                    What is it you would see?  390
If aught of woe or wonder, cease your search.
*Fort.* This quarry cries on havoc. O proud Death,
What feast is toward in thine eternal cell
That thou so many princes at a shot
So bloodily hast struck?                          395
*Ambassador.*      The sight is dismal;
And our affairs from England come too late.
The ears are senseless that should give us hearing
To tell him his commandment is fulfilled,
That Rosencrantz and Guildenstern are dead.       400
Where should we have our thanks?
*Hor.*                      Not from his mouth,
Had it the ability of life to thank you.
He never gave commandment for their death.
But since, so jump upon this bloody question,      405
You from the Polack wars, and you from England,
Are here arrived, give order that these bodies
High on a stage be placed to the view;
And let me speak to the yet unknowing world
How these things came about. So shall you hear     410
Of carnal, bloody, and unnatural acts;

421. **Which now to claim my vantage doth invite me:** which opportunity now invites me to claim

423. **whose voice will draw on more:** whose authority will attract approval by others

426. **On:** because of

429. **put on:** brought to trial

Of accidental judgments, casual slaughters;
Of deaths put on by cunning and forced cause;
And, in this upshot, purposes mistook
Fall'n on the inventors' heads. All this can I          415
Truly deliver.
    *Fort.*      Let us haste to hear it,
And call the noblest to the audience.
For me, with sorrow I embrace my fortune.
I have some rights of memory in this kingdom,          420
Which now to claim my vantage doth invite me.
    *Hor.* Of that I shall have also cause to speak,
And from his mouth whose voice will draw on more.
But let this same be presently performed,
Even while men's minds are wild, lest more mischance 425
On plots and errors happen.
    *Fort.*          Let four captains
Bear Hamlet like a soldier to the stage;
For he was likely, had he been put on,
To have proved most royally; and for his passage      430
The soldiers' music and the rites of war
Speak loudly for him.
Take up the bodies. Such a sight as this
Becomes the field, but here shows much amiss.
Go, bid the soldiers shoot.                            435
    *Exeunt marching; after the which a peal of ordnance*
                           *are shot off.*

# KEY TO

## *Famous Lines and Phrases*

For this relief much thanks.     [Francisco—I. i. 8]

... prologue to the omen coming on  [Horatio—I. i. 136]

... the morn, in russet mantle clad  [Horatio—I. i. 181]

A little more than kin and less than
 kind!           [Hamlet—I. ii. 68-9]

O that this too too solid flesh would
 melt            [Hamlet—I. ii. 135]

Frailty, thy name is woman!    [Hamlet—I. ii. 152]

In my mind's eye        [Hamlet—I. ii. 195]

A countenance more in sorrow than
 in anger.          [Horatio—I. ii. 249]

... the primrose path of dalliance  [Ophelia—I. iii. 53]

This above all: to thine own self be true [Polonius—I. iii. 82]

Something is rotten in the state of
 Denmark.       [Marcellus—I. iv. 100]

Murder most foul, as in the best it is [Ghost—I. v. 32]

Leave her to heaven      [Ghost—I. v. 93]

... one may smile, and smile, and be a
 villain          [Hamlet—I. v. 115]

*Key to Famous Lines and Phrases*

---

There are more things in heaven and
earth, Horatio,
Than are dreamt of in your
philosophy.                    [Hamlet—I. v. 191-92]

The time is out of joint. . . .        [Hamlet—I. v. 215]

. . . brevity is the soul of wit      [Polonius—II. ii. 96]

More matter, with less art.      [Queen—II. ii. 102]

Though this be madness, yet there is
method in't.            [Polonius—II. ii. 222-23]

. . . there is nothing either good or bad
but thinking makes it so.      [Hamlet—II. ii. 265-66]

What a piece of work is a man!      [Hamlet—II. ii. 319]

I am but mad north-north-west. . . .
I know a hawk from a handsaw.   [Hamlet—II. ii. 388-89]

. . . caviary to the general        [Hamlet—II. ii. 444-45]

Use every man after his desert, and
who should scape whipping?    [Hamlet—II. ii. 536-37]

O, what a rogue and peasant slave
am I!                    [Hamlet—II. ii. 556]

What's Hecuba to him, or he to
Hecuba                  [Hamlet—II. ii. 565]

. . . the devil hath power
T' assume a pleasing shape      [Hamlet—II. ii. 607-8]

The play's the thing          [Hamlet—II. ii. 612]

To be, or not to be, that is the question [Hamlet—III. i. 64]

The glass of fashion and the mould of form,
The observed of all observers   [Ophelia—III. i. 163-64]

It out-herods Herod.                     [Hamlet—III. ii. 13]

Suit the action to the word, the word
to the action                           [Hamlet—III. ii. 17-8]

The lady doth protest too much,
methinks.                               [Queen—III. ii. 243]

A king of shreds and patches!           [Hamlet—III. iv. 117]

. . . 'tis the sport to have the enginer
Hoist with his own petar                [Hamlet—III. iv. 229-30]

How all occasions do inform against
me                                      [Hamlet—IV. iv. 34]

There's such divinity doth hedge a king [King—IV. v. 132]

Alas, poor Yorick! I knew him,
Horatio.                                [Hamlet—V. i. 177-78]

Imperious Cæsar, dead and turned to
clay                                    [Hamlet—V. i. 205]

Sweets to the sweet!                    [Gertrude—V. i. 239]

There's a divinity that shapes our ends [Hamlet—V. ii. 11]

. . . there's a special providence in the
fall of a sparrow.                      [Hamlet—V. ii. 218-19]